Unmarked

LANDSCAPES ALONG HIGHWAY 16

Sarah de Leeuw

NEWEST PRESS

Library and Archives Canada Cataloguing in Publication
de Leeuw, Sarah
Unmarked : landscapes along highway 16 / Sarah de Leeuw.

ISBN 1-896300-88-X (pbk.)

1. British Columbia, Northern—Description and travel. I. Title.

FC3845.N67D4 2004   C818'.6   C2004-904869-4

Board Editor: Taiaiake Alfred
Cover and interior design: Ruth Linka
Author photograph: Linda van der Zande
Topographic maps reproduced under license from Her Majesty the Queen
in Right of Canada, with permission of Natural Resources Canada.

 Canada Council   Conseil des Arts Canadian Patrimoine
for the Arts   du Canada   Heritage   canadien

NeWest Press acknowledges the support of the Canada Council for the Arts
and the Alberta Foundation for the Arts, and the Edmonton Arts Council for
our publishing program. We also acknowledge the financial support of the
Government of Canada through the Book Publishing Industry Development
Program (BPIDP) for our publishing activities.

NeWest Press
201–8540–109 Street
Edmonton, Alberta T6G 1E6
(780) 432-9427
www.newestpress.com

1   2   3   4   5   07   06   05   04

NeWest Press is committed to protecting the environment and to the responsible
use of natural resources. This book is printed on 100% post-consumer recycled
and ancient-forest-friendly paper. For more information please visit
www.oldgrowthfree.com.

PRINTED AND BOUND IN CANADA

This book is dedicated to the memory of Theresa Newhouse,

without whom the landscapes of northern British Columbia

would never have shone so brightly.

TABLE OF CONTENTS

I REMEMBER THE MOMENT WELL.

I was eight years old and my father in a suit was a rare sight. It was a fall day in 1982, my mother helped him knot his tie, and there was discussion of him making a flight on time. For the next few days, the phone rang at awkward times. It would ring in the middle of dinner or when my mother was putting us to bed, but because I was young I did not pay much attention to what was being discussed. On the evening of the third day my father returned with the news that he'd landed a job and, although he was not wearing a suit, I also remember that moment well. It was the moment that I understood movement, the moment I understood concepts of passage and journeying, of moving from one place to another, far away.

In an attempt to make sense of the move, my parents showed me a map, pointing out a red dot in the lower left-hand corner of British Columbia that represented where our house was then. Slowly my father traced the thin line leading from our red dot towards the top of the page. His finger paused at smaller dots along the way and he mentioned place names I had never heard of. His finger passed lakes and rivers, crossed bridges, and zigzagged through mountain ranges. It never stopped in its climb towards the top of the page. Somewhere near the top his finger began to move towards the left again, this time towards the huge ocean with the word *Pacific* etched onto its surface. His finger stopped for a moment at the edge of the ocean as he explained about the long ferry ride we would take to the islands where his new job was. We would ride in a boat bigger than our house,

1

he explained, and we would move with our dogs and cats and my sister and everything we owned to those islands in the Pacific Ocean.

"Right here," he said. "This is where your new school will be," and his finger circled a space as green as all the other green space on those two islands.

"Where is the red dot?" I asked, and he answered that the town we were moving to was not big enough for a red dot or, for that matter, a dot of any colour. My eyes fixed on an unmarked spot of the mapped landscape where my father's finger rested.

The road my father's finger traced, a line between Prince George and Port Clements, has come to define the landscape of my home. I have discovered this landscape by working for logging camps and women's centres, for truck stops and newspapers, for schools and grocery stores, restaurants and museums. Residents have a keen eye for detail; they are able to relate accounts of their history and geography with brilliance, humour, and empathy. Could anyone know better how to detail the many truths of a town, or the stretch of a road, than a woman who has walked those places late on a winter evening with three children in tow? Perhaps no one knows better the realties of a hinterland existence, of the boom and bust cycles of a logging community, than an ex-faller turned truck driver who tells of his life over a truck stop countertop.

In my mind, story of place is inseparable from geography of place. The telling of stories is the creation of maps, words following a finger tracing the thin red lines of roads, the curvatures of topographic lines, the stories of landscapes passed through and passed on.

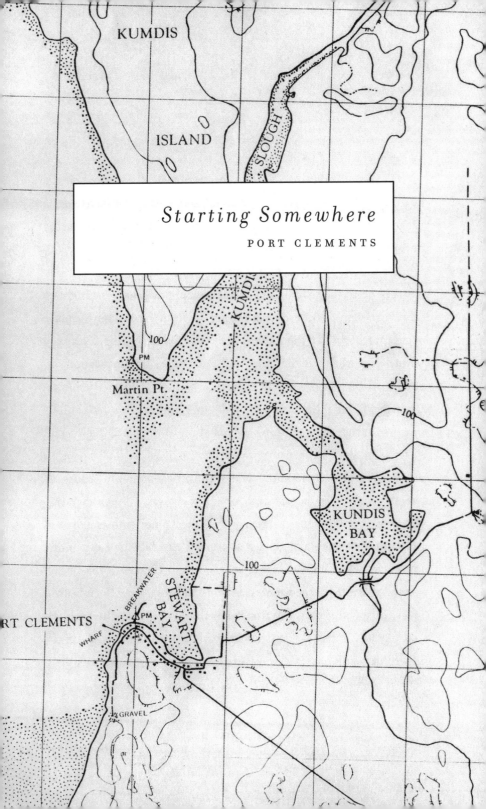

KUMDIS

ISLAND

SLOUGH

Starting Somewhere
PORT CLEMENTS

KUNDI

100

PM

Martin Pt.

100

KUNDIS
BAY

100

BREAKWATER

STEWART
BAY

RT CLEMENTS

PM

WHARF

GRAVEL

IT STARTS SOMEWHERE.

It must. Everything has a beginning after all, even when the beginning denotes only something missed—a skipped heartbeat, a breath hesitated, a head turned back, something surely moving in the periphery.

But where? Where does it begin?

A bend in the road or a particular telephone pole? The highway kilometre sign? White letters on green, letting you know a place occurs further down the road; this might be a beginning, a starting point. Or perhaps at the announcement of its (un)incorporation: small white sign, black letters reading "Port Clements: Unincorporated." No date, no population number. This is definitely one beginning, the beginning for instance, of my mother's work in Port Clements. The unincorporated sign might be as good a place as any to begin. I remember clearly the once-a-month Thursday evening rush as my mother prepared for the city council meeting. She was the municipal secretary. Not clerk, not transcriber, not assistant: just secretary. Once a month she carefully typed the minutes of a town hall meeting, the words of Port Clement's mayor and council in neatly aligned sentences and columns. To get the job she'd had to do a typing test. The first time around she was so nervous she laid her hands across the typewriter and placed her fingers on the incorrect row of letters, typing a dictated memo in nonsense words. They let her do the test again because no other applicants had come in for the position.

STARTING SOMEWHERE: PORT CLEM

So this beginning springs forth from confusion; it's muddled. Perhaps a better place to begin is Jack's house.

This seems clearer, if only because everyone selects a right hand turn or a left hand turn at Jack's house, situated as it is at the crossroads of Port Clements. Turn left and you go downtown, if one could say Port Clements has a downtown. Turn right and you head out of town, towards Masset and the army base an hour down the highway. His house is balanced mere steps from the unincorporated sign, as if punctuating municipal pride. By the time I was in grade five, Jack had a new home. Two others had burned down, and now a trailer sat jacked up on blocks, kept off the ground to make sure it did not rust too much. Its walls were already eaten through, great brown holes gaping so that in places the guts of his home were visible through the siding.

Everyone knows that when you see Jack's place you have made the drive home to Port Clements. His house announces home, declares for residents that just around the corner their own warm rooms rest in wait. The yard is a miserable chaos of junk, items waging silent war against each other in painful contortions of twisted metal, snapped wood, ripped plastic, and bent wire and cable. Look closely and what you see is Jack's life piled in front of this trailer. Countless motors from unidentifiable machines (lawn mowers, tractors, boats?) peek from beneath blue plastic tarps coated in fallen red cedar needles. Five cars, or the skeletons of what once were cars, squat like abstract sculptures. Tires and mufflers piled on top of fenders, these in turn piled on top of hoods. Only one of those cars runs, but Jack always swore it paid off to keep the bodies of others on hand, just in case something might need to be fixed.

5

Once, years ago, Jack had decided to carve burls. To make a little extra money on the side, he said. The burls now lay in haphazard heaps, thick contortions of deformity chain-sawed from trees; wooden bodies resting against the corpses of cars. Centre sections of the occasional burl are carved out, a testimony to Jack's plan to sell burl salad bowls to tourists. Other burls have been thinly sliced—now faceless future burl clocks dull from never knowing a thick varnish coat.

Jack's house is a good beginning. It speaks of continual loss yet infinite hope, an absolute certainty that in nothing there exists something. His house opens a door to the town of Port Clements, a town that can be missed in the blink of an eye, driven past because you have turned your head, distracted for a moment by a bend in the road or a scent you could not quite place. A scent of ocean on log booms, the scent of a dry land sort, quiet in the evening air.

Early on it became apparent I lived in a passed-by town, a town easily missed. Before I lived there, before I came to know it, it was unknown to everyone, even me. At the age of eight, to my grade three teacher, I announced my family was moving.

"Where?" asked the teacher, and I recall the eyes of my classmates on me, a sharp inhale of air held in expectation.

"Port Clements," I answered. Silence settled around the room, and the teacher asked me once again, as if by rephrasing the question a community would appear, as if by my answering a second time a place of meaning would come into focus, some town that could be recalled even if it had not ever been visited, seen, or committed to memory from experience. So many of these places exist, places known from the images captured of them, known from the discussion had about them. The town I was moving to was not such a place.

"Port Clements," I restated.

"Ou est ca?" asked Monsieur Longe, because even in my French immersion classroom, even in another language, the town was foreign.

"It's on the Queen Charlotte Islands," I told my classmates, and the teacher smiled, a place he knew finally coming clear.

"Oh," said Monsieur Longe. "I hear it never stops raining there."

Indeed, we crossed to the islands through mist and rain, my sister, mother, and me. My father had gone on ahead, manoeuvring the great bulk of the moving truck north from southern BC and Vancouver Island, away from my classmates who knew nothing of my new community, away from cities and towns whose names everyone knew. The roads we drove to arrive at the ferry left cities behind, vast swaths of trees and barrenness became increasingly common, and my mother's anxious calculation of miles between gas stations spoke of spaces empty and endlessly alone.

My memory of journeying is vivid. Clusters of towns thinning out into open fields and sage covered hills, the scent of ocean far behind. My mother reciting the names of places I have never heard of: Spuzzum, Hell's Gate, Merritt, Cache Creek. This is the interior of British Columbia, miles and miles of undulation and curving landscape. Then Hundred Mile House, my sister and I playing name games: Williams Lake, caught a snake; Quesnel, Quesnel, oh well, oh well. Here our journey itself curved, back towards the coast and westward, the possibility of sea-scent once again real. Hills stretched into flatness and lowlands, then Prince George, Burns Lake, then back into mountains and Smithers, the hush of new snow, even this early, even in late August.

These mountains, my mother is saying, are the edge of an ancient sea, all of this was once underwater, and we are taken with images of starfish on cedar trees, silver fish abutting with logging trucks, rainforest in an impossible coral reef, as impossible as the journey itself. I am lost in the hours it has taken to travel this far; two days of driving and only on this second day does nearness become real. We are near the coast again, near a new point of departure.

Achieving our place by travelling the remains of ancient oceans.

Before this my world was contained and I did not understand size, the impossibility of moving so far and achieving so little. I was young and the careful mapping I had done included paths to school, roads leading to my grandparents, the small tract of land at the bottom of my street, the edge of fence across which I reached to feed carrots to horses. Contained. Moving north uprooted me, left me groundless in the face of so much land. I am floating on an ancient sea, travelling to my new home, a place unknown by those who knew me.

Beyond Smithers, there are place names my eight-year-old tongue trips on. Kitsegukla, Kitwanga. The turn off to Kitwancool, Gitanyow, the Alaskan Highway. I ask at every bend, have we arrived? I am impatient, needing to know everything immediately. Where we will live, what my school will look like, even the colour of my bedroom walls is a question. Moricetown. Here? Is this our destination? New Hazelton? Terrace? The highway is endless. I am sure we are the only people on the road and nothing exists anymore; my previous yard, the small place behind the back fence and between the white garden shed, the tree branch located exactly seven knotholes from the ground. Against the highway, against the possibility of a new home, everything fades.

Then, Prince Rupert. The great mountains are far away, the ocean is real, not ancient and imaginary, and we will cross it in the mist and rain on a great white boat winging through the water, the horn shaking down my spine, sleeping in a room of such wonder, swallowed into the bowels of the great ship, perfectly dark when the lights are shut out. To get to my new home, you have to sleep twice, awaken two mornings in a row to a horizon you have never seen.

My new home is not a location; it is distance.

I am expecting something different, a visual reminder that these people are three days travel and two nights sleep away from the people I have left behind. I stare hard. My mind insists they are strangers, unknown, living in a place on the edge of nothingness. I know I have moved to a place on the edge of nothingness because I hear it spoken of as such by people who come and visit my parents, people who come from cities with names I find on the globe in my grade three classroom.

My father's friends come to hunt. No place better, they laugh. You can bag a deer a day; play steelhead from dawn to dusk. Couldn't live here though, oh no, how do you do it anyway? Missed the place driving in, thought it was a highway camp or something, because surely it wasn't a whole town. Surely that speck couldn't be it, not the whole damn place. Got forty clicks out when we checked the odometer, and sure as shit, we realized we'd passed right through. Had to turn around on the highway, almost clocked a bear right then and there. Place is just crawling with them, you might as well be living on top of them. Great place to come hunting, sure is, but no way we could live here.

For two and half weeks my sister and I find candy bars under our

pillows. My father's two friends chide my parents. How are you supposed to bring up kids here? That isn't a school they've got, it might
as well be an outbuilding. Only goes to grade six—then what, the bus?
Two and half hours a day on the bus? In the city they'd never have to
go through that.

On the back porch covered in tin roofing with the rain beating
down in our forgotten town, deer hang, meat softening. My sister and
I know how to skin and gut a deer: it hangs from its back legs and you
cut from its genitals towards the throat, peeling back the skin, slicing
the white membrane that attaches hide to flesh. You slice down the
inside of the chest cavity, carefully pulling out the innards, feeding
gut and intestine to the dogs, saving the heart, liver, and kidney to fry
for dinner, fat popping on the stove.

We learn this in our passed-by town, in the off hours, when we
are not attending our outbuilding school, when we have stopped
dreaming of cities and the places where we once lived. We learn it
with our hands deep in the chest cavities of deer; guts still warm as we
think of pavement and skyscrapers and knowing we are not there by
knowing all that is raw and thick within freshly killed game.

Port Clements has no place to buy school supplies, no place to
register for and take swimming lessons, no galleries, no restaurants
to dine in, no place to watch a movie, no police officers, no malls, no
civic centre, no doctor's office, no corner stores, no video stores or
clothing stores, nor a single chain-named business.

An attempt is made.

Two churches, though we attend neither. A community hall with
Christmas concerts and once, just once, a movie brought in. The
entire town on splintered chairs scraping varnished wood floor,

sawdust from red-strap jeans flickers in the blue light. *Tron*. I understand none of it, but it makes no difference. The movie is only part of why we are here. The idea of it is everything. Nothing else truly exists other than for the idea of it.

One store, with no fresh fruit and a back section with dusty jigsaw puzzles and plastic dolls in brittle plastic wrap. Everyone knows birthday gifts must be ordered weeks in advance from the Sears catalogue. Who would dream of buying the outdated merchandise in Bay View Market? A gas station. A bank opens one afternoon a week in a building that was once Federal Fisheries down by the dock. The bank teller comes in from out of town, from the big city two hours away, the one with a single high school. She wears red high-heeled shoes, a belt around her waist, and is the greatest fashion icon we have in Port Clements. One hotel, where loggers come to stay when they get out of camp, days off spent before the television, beer balanced on windowsills.

By Grade Four I know my town by what it is not, by the vacancies and gaps it could not fill. The red house located in that gap, two exits past the dump on the way out of town, a stone's throw from the gravel pit, and just on the edge of a clear cut, this red house is the location of my childhood. My feet remain welded firmly to the ground of a town overlooked.

From that red house, if you peddled fast, terribly fast so that your feet got going quicker than the pedals, you could make the sharp bend, the one down the hill and past the Golden Spruce Hotel, and you could make it in a way that stole your breath. The bike pedal was a filament of space from the pavement, and the slightest miscalculation would leave you bruised on the edge of Kumdis Slough, a wind from the tidal flats sickly rotten in your lungs. If you twisted through that curve though, perfectly balanced, the one main road of Port Clements opened its beaten pavement arms to you. Past an intersection—the terrible intersection with the boy who squashed orange and black caterpillars, an alder branch carefully cut for the purpose, flattened and sanded on one end, the better to catch body between stick and pavement—past the Mac and Blow machinist shop, grader perpetually parked outside, someone always working on it. Then those nice houses, the four on the hill to the left, new and company-built, the homes of fallers and foremen, the turn-off to the school and the Ministry of Highway's storage lots, the wet pitted baseball field, the tackle and hunting shop and Sears order counter all in one.

If you negotiated that steep curve, everything became possible, again and again.

Over the bridge, the waters of Kumdis Creek brown under the thickly creosoted deck. On the right hand side, a CN Rail worker from Quebec lived in a trailer court with four trailers. I knew because I babysat for his kids; someone in town heard I spoke a few words of French. On Friday nights, once a month, I put the two children of the displaced CN Rail worker to bed.

"Bon nuit," I would say. "Bon voyage."

I had forgotten how to say "sweet dreams" in French, and in the silence of a logging camp town I sent those children into the night journeying. The beginning of something, even if translated incorrectly, in a lapsed language.

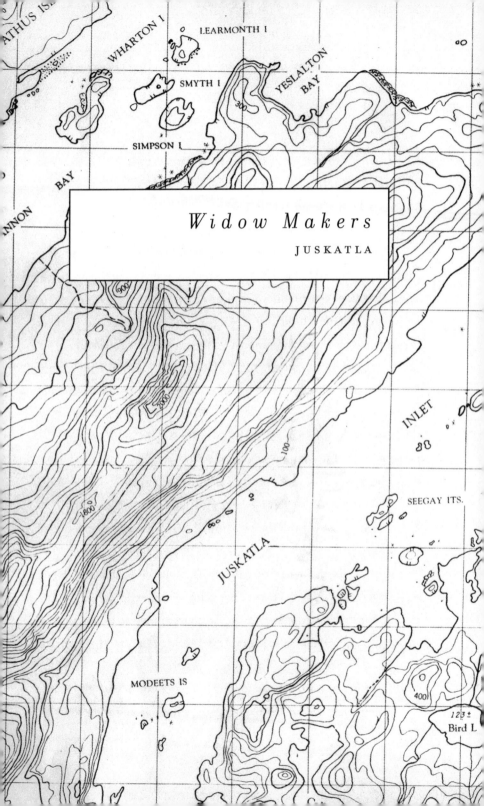

Widow Makers
JUSKATLA

Learning to smoke entailed stealing Sportsmen unfiltered cigarettes from Leaha's dad on Friday nights.

After he'd passed out following a week of choker setting, of course.

We could take them directly from his shirt pocket; once, pressing the snap closed so hard on his cowboy style shirt that the pressure seemed to dent his ribs inward, him not moving an inch, his deep breathing unaltered. Friday nights meant that there were men throughout trailer and bunkhouse rooms in Juskatla falling into the same state as Leaha's dad, most of the guys staying drunk until Monday morning, many not yet sober as they pulled on their red-strap jeans well before 5:00 AM, lifting Husquavarna chainsaws onto their shoulders, one saw for each side. They would work a drunk off, booze slipping out of their pores while they made the day's first cuts, deep and perfectly slanted into the sides of Sitka spruce, always hoping like hell not to meet a widow maker, that freak tree that might at any time snap out with all the pressure of so many hundreds of years, easily shattering a man, breaking life in a single mean moment.

Men like Leaha's dad were men with hands wrecked from bush work and faces that bore scars of being broken open in bar fights and busted down in logging accidents. These were men with the skin of monsters, burned from chainsaw diesel spilling behind their collars as they packed saws while walking from crummies into the bush. Leaha's father epitomized the broken body of a Juskatla logging man. By the mid-eighties, he had been logging with Mac and Blow for over twenty years. To show for it he walked with a bent and painful drag, was missing most every one of his teeth, and had a gold Cadillac with white leather seats and a double wide trailer balanced on the edge of a gravel road. That Cadillac was his pride and joy, gold flashing against gravel, white leather against scars and breakings.

Every good bender began with a bottle of Canadian Club in one hand, a bucket of Turtle Wax "wash and wax in one" solution in the other. Right after work, even though supper was waiting and a fight always flared up red-hot between him and his wife when he chose the gold Cadillac over her, he would wash the week's grime from that vehicle, inch by inch with the care one might take to administer medication to a deathly ill child. And then the slow logger's drunk would overtake him, carefully like all logger drunks do, and the man would get gentle and slow, an escape from work that ruined him, leaving him with nothing but his own slow escape.

In grade five we stole cigarettes from a man who drove his gold Cadillac fast over back roads, set chokers during the day, and drank himself to oblivion in the evenings. No one seemed to notice when Leaha and I climbed out the side door and slipped down to the mess house and bunk houses and machinists's yards where we crouched in the metal jaws of front end loaders and taught ourselves to inhale. Only seven kids lived in the logging camp of Juskatla, so even when I came to stay with Leaha we were easy to overlook. And those easy to overlook have a freedom to view as they please, which is just what Leaha and I did.

Smells hard to describe exist in logging camps, smells neither sweet nor acrid occupy a place in memory painfully difficult to clearly position and, failing that, to eliminate. The smells shift throughout the day, starting early in the morning with propane as camp stoves are lit, bacon grease, then the piss and filth of loggers waking up and converging in shared bathroom stalls in bunkhouses. By mid-afternoon the scents have slid smoothly into the realm of fabric softener as load after load of Stanfield sweaters and GWG red-strap jeans are washed, into the realm of hot welded metal as in-camp mechanics solder trucks and loaders, and, finally, into roasting meat as the camp prepares for its returning men. Then first up in the evening is a thick odour of diesel from returning crummy trucks, then a haze of cedar sawdust scent followed by an indescribable scent of men's sweat mingling with food. Late into the night, a scent cloud of burning wood hangs over the camp, and to this the silent smell of men at rest is added. This smell, the smell of loggers at rest, of hand-rolled cigarettes and damp newspapers, dirty sheets and pots of weak coffee, these are the scents that greeted Leaha and me when, after dinner, we snuck through Atco trailer halls of thin brown-panelled wood walls, dashing into non-occupied rooms as the floor squeaked warnings of loggers on the move. The scent of ancient Louis L'Amour duster novels piled pile upon pile. Hustler magazines tossed into bathroom stalls, shards of Irish Spring soap used and forgotten, caught in the tiled corners of bunkhouse bathrooms.

We shared the air with loggers home from falling, from bucking and loading. We breathed in the spaces they forgot to look. We watched them doing nothing at all. It was everything to us.

Scents suggest silence, as if the camp operated in a vapour of smell isolated from any other senses. Nothing could be farther from the truth. Sound erupted from between every piece of stored machinery, from beside every bunkhouse and mess hall, from the dark insides of every company-owned trailer in Juskatla. Sound is the glue of a logging camp, the thick foam insulation squeezed and expanding into every corner, filling in the cracks and back eddies, fat on bones. How did we know this? How did sound come to fill our ears, fan itself out from our ears through our veins?

Leaha and I knew this because it was the sound of someone being broken that drew us to Davie Junior's trailer on the Thursday night of a long weekend. Sound, and the fact that Davie Junior was just one grade ahead of us and already a practiced smoker, drew us across a gravel road flowing with rain and mud. We had known that wandering until the early morning hours around Juskatla with Davie Junior would ensure excitement and possibility. We knew this even as we heard the ripping sounds of air filled with fighting between adult and child. We simply waited outside and listened as his father flew at him. No wall could contain the wails. But no doors opened in camp, Davie's dad being a foreman and all.

Years later, the twelve-year-old face of Davie would creep into the edges of my memory, a face red and pulped as a rotting nurse log; no tears though, no tears for a boy who would go on to be a logger.

From wails to the song of a strong break as loggers began an evening of pool, the sound of truck tires revved fast and resolved on gravel driveways, the echoes of men yelling at each other, of dogs barking from unspecified sites. These are logging camp melodies, heard against a sky reflecting clearcuts.

Nothing escaped our ears, not the shifting bodies of men as they slept in beds too small, not the midnight wanderings of a man having the last cigarette of his day. To us it seemed the only silence of

Juskatla was the silence that accompanied a lack of women. Fewer than twenty families lived in camp, so mostly it was a landscape of men and their sounds. Not a single woman lived in the bunkhouses, their voices unheard in any of the machine shops or mess houses—here it was the sound of loggers, and women didn't log.

Though Leaha's mother rarely left the house, stepping out only twice a month to head into "town," the tiny cluster of Port Clements with its elementary school, one store, and no bank, she nonetheless had a formidable impact on Leaha and me. It was Leaha's mother, after all, and not Leaha's father, who caught us returning one night through the side door of the trailer. It was Leaha's mother who had patiently waited with metal spoon in hand until we crept home well past 1:00 AM and who then flew at Leaha in a deadly quiet anger so rendered and carefully concentrated that it left Leaha with seventy-seven bruises. I received not a single mark, through I witnessed the metal spoon smashing at Leaha and heard with absolute clarity Leaha's mother as she spoke softly, almost gently, saying over and over to Leaha, "Do you want to end up a slut in a logging camp? Is that what you want? To be a slut in a logging camp?" I have no memory of tears one way or the other. Leaha may have cried, but then again she may not have. What I do remember are the welts rising up on Leaha's skin, blood blisters where the edge of the spoon came close to breaking the skin but proved not quite sharp enough.

Roaming a logging camp, knowing a company-owned town, a community suspended on the edge of being nothing, leaves blisters and boils just beneath the skin's surface.

Though dullness saved Leaha's skin from scars, it certainly did not save the community of Juskatla from damage and eventual eradication. By 1986, lethargy had sunk deep into the veins of the logging industry on the Queen Charlotte Islands. Men talked of days gone by, days when the sounds of push sticks on logging booms sitting fat and ripened in the waters of Juskatla Inlet were the sounds of everyday. Days when the numbers etched deep into a scaler's stick were worn thin in no time at all, a scaler had that much work for him. Days when a logger could quit and find work within hours, days past when a logger could have a fight with a foreman and walk back hat in hand to that same job a day later because a need existed for loggers. Days past.

They talked about past days and watched the dismantlement of Juskatla, pot by pot, mattress by mattress, bunkhouse shaving mirror by bunkhouse shaving mirror.

Leaha and I had learned to inhale by then. I think social services had made their first calls to her house; some discussions were circling in the air about foster families. The last night of Juskatla was the last night I ever spent at Leaha's house. Her bruises had long ago healed and my parents were not aware of beatings with metal spoons and somehow this is all welded together in my mind with the night a logging town shut down.

Perhaps it is pain fused with pain, bruise with bruise. The sound of a metal spoon smashing against skin, the sound of an auctioneer. "I have ten, do I hear fifteen, fifteen, do I hear twenty?" This for great slabs of stainless steel counter, a cookhouse—piece by stainless steel piece. This for grapple yarding cable, great rust-coloured coils of it, thicker than my twelve year old wrist. For chainsaws sold by the dozen, for tools and engines and lanterns and every piece of something and nothing upon which logging camps run, upon which communities build themselves.

This for mattresses indented with the shapes of a sleeping logger's body.

Five days and four nights they auctioned off Juskatla, piece by piece, great spotlights catching the steam of onlookers's breath, inhale, exhale, a way of life sold off. And I remember clearly the look of Leaha's father, Sportsmen Unfiltered cigarette cradled gently between fingers, sitting legs apart, elbows on knees, on the hood of his gold Cadillac.

A stunned look of resignation, the same look I had always imagined might flash across a faller's face the instant he cut into a widow maker, those terrible trees who in such a long split second rip out to take a man down.

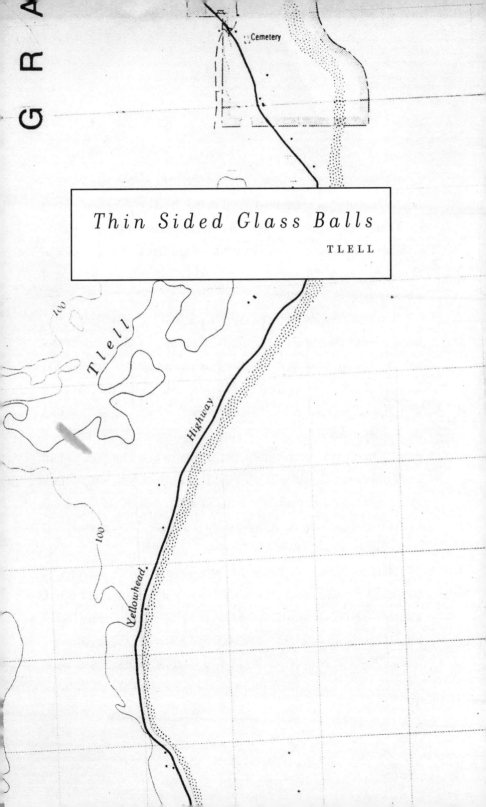

Thin Sided Glass Balls

TLELL

Perhaps we believed the miles of ocean, wave on wave on wave, would somehow alleviate a hush of tension, a cloying residue of guilt or sadness. As if in that loud emptiness of sea on sand and trees leaning into wind, our own smallness would be amplified and our troubles become small, insignificant. Once a walk to Ship Wreck at the far end of Tlell's beaches followed the shooting of a bear.

Early on a Friday afternoon, my sister and I were walking home from school. I was pushing a bike, bright blue, and my sister was wearing a hot pink skirt, ridiculously short, and fighting off mosquitoes and black flies, a sure sign of mid-June. We are following the well charted paths of children in a logging town, making our way past the tiny apartment block where single men stay when they're not in camp, making our way past the rotting carcasses of hauling equipment and crummies with their motors cradled in hydraulic lifts to their sides, past the gavel pit where coils of iron cable thicker than our wrists rest in puddles slick with rainbow gas and flakes of rust, past the dump turnoff where everyone goes to watch bears.

Memory makes up truths for you, so perhaps at the precise moment we heard shots ring out we were not musing about bears, great black bodies against black garbage bags stinking sweet and sickly in the sun. And a great black body falling in our shed, our Joeyshack. The first shot stops us, a quick instinctual reaction to drop down and take cover, some other far-away memory of bullets flying through trees, hunters unaware of a family walking through the forest, my father lying spread eagled on top of his two daughters, my mother, face pressed into moss and dirt, my father screaming stop, stop, there are people here, stop shooting, and the thin high whistle of bullets through hemlock trees. For a moment the loud crack seems like a mistake, a once off imagined, and we are looking towards our house, only a minute or two away, and wondering aloud if we imagined the shot, or if it is really coming from our house, our house now right in front of us. Then the air fractures again, and again, and once more in rapid succession, crackings and bangs so loud we feel them for a moment dislodge our breath and heartbeat, sounds so deafening and thick they are as if someone has lifted us, shaking our bodies, letting us fall to the ground unbalanced.

Where do we run as children hearing gunshots? Home, the place where gunshots are not supposed to originate, and so we are running, the short steps from the other side of the road to our driveway and around the corner across the mossy lawn and up to our backdoor, and straight into the bodies of men, four unknown men and our father, each of them holding fast to a corner of a recently dead and still warm black bear, head lolling to the side, blood from the corner of its mouth, our dogs jumping crazily, not barking, frenzied beyond bark-ing. I recall the slack weight of black bear muscle in my hand. My father, two conservation officers, two policemen, standing beside the carcass, considering carefully how to lift well over 800 pounds of dead weight into the back of a pickup truck. My hands pushed deep into the fur of a dead bear, my palm even today feeling his still warm innards, the settling of guts to the side, the muscle between leg bones, the thick dullness of a single claw, useless and caked with mud. I am even able to lift up his lip, wet and soft rubbery, teeth still slick with saliva and blood, it is now I take note of the bottom jaw, missing and scabbed, curved around the shape of an old bullet wound. A bear left to starve, foraging in the Joey-shack lilting off our house, desperate for jars of huckleberry jam, canned salmon, and potatoes from our garden. A starving bear no parents want their child colliding with at 3:20 on a Friday afternoon.

All evening my father is despondent. He lies on the couch, hand and arm dropping off the edge, fingers brushing the floor, eyes staring at the ceiling. Our dogs lick his wrist, but still he does not stir, makes no move to scratch behind their ears, rub their bellies. Our father is preoccupied with the killing of a bear, and my sister and I orbit about him, asking him things about beaches, about agates and stones we have wondered about all week. We have recently received a rock polisher, a mechanical barrel that runs day in and day out, a background noise of churning rocks and working motor, a sound years later my father tells us kept him awake for nights on end. Like a combination of washing machine and ocean, mechanized waves on rocks.

Perhaps it was the need to forget recent death, culpability in the ending of a being's life. Perhaps it was my sister's and my desire to polish more translucent orange agates and rough red beach rock.

The next morning we drove towards open ocean, miles of sand punctuated with tufts of razor-sharp beach grass, refugee logs escaped from logging booms, salted silver and smooth. The spit in front of us and to our left, we are driving south along Highway 16, my father offering his favourite answer to our "are we there yet" question, him saying it's right around the corner, but it's a long, long corner, so you won't know it has ended until we get there. Through muskeg bogs with stunted pine trees, creeks the colour of tea, rusty water, water that stains rocks. Along the way I talk about the kids I go to school with, the ones from Tlell, each and every one of them smells like salt, we all know it at school, pointing at them, knowing their parents are hippies. Only hippies live in Tlell, with the exception of our grade four teacher, the one no one dares talk back to because her last name is Bitterlich, and her husband is German.

It does not need to make sense; we have invented horror stories. Once it rushed around the school that her husband planted the bomb found on a Tlell beach. Her daughter and two friends were riding horses on the beach when they found it. Mrs. Bitterlich lived on a farm in Tlell, the only teacher we know of on the islands who rode horses, sometimes wearing riding boots into the classroom. Resting beside her teacher's desk was a hard riding hat, plastic showing through black velvet where, at the hat's edges, the material was pulled tight.

Amongst the driftwood and clam shells and sea gravel, an old wwii bomb, sides bashed in, fin tails like a comic-book drawing of a spaceship, but one snapped off. For weeks everyone was fascinated with the bomb. At birthday parties we told stories of a child from Skidegate reserve having her arm blown off. We chart the entire incident, down to the fine spray of blood fanning out with the Sou'wester windstorm we know must have been raging.

Nautical maps and ocean currents mean nothing to us. We invent the beaches of Tlell.

We are sure the wwii bomb is German. How could it be anything else? We do not listen to truths; our invented Tlell beaches are rife with Germans and hidden artillery. Our teacher's husband organizes them, we are sure. Once I asked my mother about the bomb. She stated matter-of-factly that the men from the army base in Masset removed it the day after it was found, discovered it was dud, and hauled it off to the dump. She explained briefly about currents from Japan washing things up onto the beaches of Tlell, how sometimes blowfish from the tropics were discovered, their bloated bodies more dangerous than any spent and expended bomb. We talked for a moment about the carcass of a white shark discovered on the west coast of South Moresby, the most northerly white shark to have ever been found.

I forget the shark is dead, going to school the next day, and later to another birthday party, and spread the word. I add to the stories of German bombs the tales of cold Tlell waters filled with schools of deadly white sharks, appetites sharpened after being separated for so long from schools of Japanese fish. I elaborate where necessary, telling anyone within ear shot about white sharks swallowing motorboats. About white sharks being hauled up in the nets of trawlers and gill-netters, great scale-covered jaws clamping down on the legs of fishermen, limbs flying into the inky black waters of Hecate Straight. I create details each time I tell the story. My stories become part of the school landscape, worked into the minds of children who refuse to walk the beaches with their parents. A mother complains. My own parents wonder why I have to lie when the truth was so clearly spelled out to me. I cannot explain that the truth holds no interest for me. That the lands and events I imagine are much more real than army personnel efficiently dealing with spent bomb casings, much more interesting than ravens eating slowly from the body of a great white shark silently resting on sand.

When my family walks the beaches of Tlell, we weave between

sand and forest, the beach trickling into moss and red cedar trees, salted driftwood taken over by lady ferns and salal. We know the walk ends in a shipwreck, so we are not searching for forgotten ships and chests of undiscovered treasure. But we carry bags nonetheless. Plastic grocery bags from the Masset Co-Op food store, each of us with at least two, one for each pocket. My father likes to fill his with Chantrelle mushrooms, their pungent orange bodies fat in the sand-heavy, moss-covered soil of rainforest abutting on beach. Sometimes my sister and I rush down hills on the right-hand side of the path, tearing off Witch's Hair lichen as we compete to get the most mushrooms—heedless of smoothing moss back into place, we rip at the ground, wrapping our hands around the gilled flesh.

We fill our bags with rocks, agates being the ultimate find. They are like brains, pock-marked and veiny, sometimes white, sometimes orange, sometimes watery yellow, and once, only once, a pale green the colour of mist. At home our rooms are filed with jars of agates, boxes of agates, agates on the windowsill, agates on the edges of bookcases. My sister and I harbour a wistful lust that one day agates will be declared more than a semi-precious stone, that one day the rocks of Tlell beaches will be seen for their true worth, and, by a slip of coincidence, we will be rich, rich enough to order diamonds and gold from the Sears Catalogue.

The bags my mother carries are never heavy. Always, it seems, they are light as if only filled with air. In her bag she puts feathers, long, speckled feathers of young eagles, deep purpley-black feathers of ravens, grey and white gull feathers, sandy beige feathers, down feathers of sand skipper birds or ducks that rest between the tufts of grass. On occasion, she deviates from feathers and picks up the odd sand dollar or bits of coloured glass. When she puts these in her bags of feathers, they fall to the bottom slowly, resting for a time on the feathers like buoyant dry logs on the surface of the Pacific Ocean.

Once, when our family walked the beaches of Tlell in January, the sky ripped open against grey ocean waters. On that January afternoon the rain fell with such force it bit into our skin. We held our hands against our faces, looking for all the world as if we were praying as we hiked. Our grandparents were with us that time, visiting over the holidays and into the New Year. We had walked for almost two hours when we came to a slice in the beach, a rusty coloured stream pouring from the forest in a bloated rush, displacing sand in a hungry flurry, devouring our path. I remember my Opa whistling Bach, silently conducting a private orchestra, and my father carrying each of us in turn over the stream, my Opa the last to cross, not being carried, but carefully supported, the sand pushed by water and meeting his ankles to form moraines, instant geological phenomena. That walk was conceived to quiet the tensions between generations, to soothe comments made by grandparents, misunderstood by grandchildren, and translated by brittle parents exhausted from the efforts of carefully navigating tenuous connections of love and family.

Together we become small, an open ocean reaching to Japan dwarfing our troubles, making invisible our concerns and differences, billions of sand grains moving against trees resisting a vicious sky.

As the rain bit our skin, we searched for storm agates and kept our eyes peeled for glass balls, the ultimate prize of any beach-combing expedition. We sipped tea inside the walls of Tlell's shipwreck, the bow pointing everlastingly towards the sky, a portal gazing vertical.

Did we remember, asked my mother, the time we came to Tlell last, just after a storm, and we found two glass balls, one still encased in netting, one so worn from revolving in waves against invisible particulates that, by touching it, we risked shattering its thin glass sides. That once, just once during that trip, my mother lifted the thin-walled glass ball from the sand and placed it in her bag of feathers. Together we walked parallel to the sea, forgetting everything but the sand and the sky and the desperately breakable moments and fragile possessions that we all find ourselves momentarily in charge of.

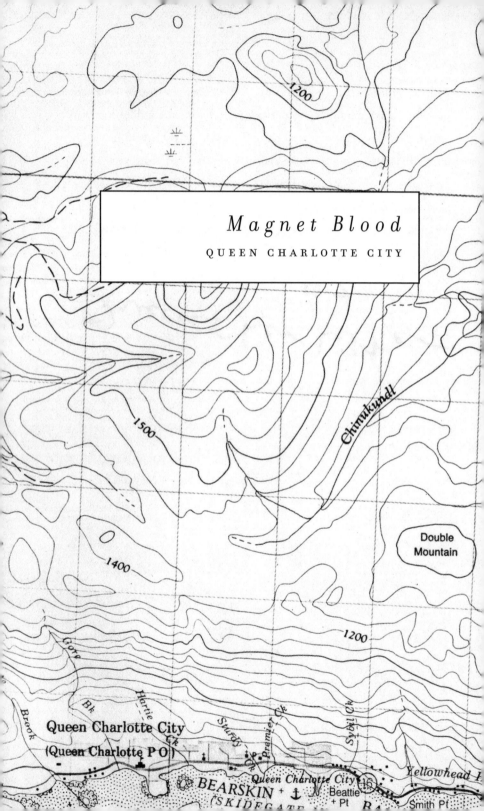

Magnet Blood

QUEEN CHARLOTTE CITY

NOT UNTIL MANY YEARS LATER DO I COME TO KNOW that living here was living in a land so real and raw that it slipped into the impossible, a land of legends not to be believed, a place of things not real. No one believes the tales I have to tell, the tales of balancing rocks and whales spitting on highways. Of road fissures so deep that a constant stream of cement cannot fill them, tiny earthquakes always re-opening the pavement. Drink from the water near this fracture and your blood will be charged like a magnet; you will always return, a compass needle veering towards the magnetic north. Sometimes the need to return will fill you with a draw so urgent your teeth will chatter and the joints in your body will ache. As a teenager I stood below watchmen with human bones at their base, I held the colours of gas-on-water in my hand, abalone shells laughingly resting in the place of my eyes and mouth. In my mind I became a creature of the sea, rising from the waves breaking forever on the shores of those mist-enclosed jewel islands that no one but a few called home.

Return I did, my joints aching until my feet touched the ground at Skidegate Landing. It was now long past those once endless nights between the age of eleven and fifteen when we wandered the only main street, the only paved street, dreaming of sweaters knit with gold thread and hanging in the window of Brown's Store in the Skidegate reserve, an ancients store built on the beach next to the Band Office with fallen totems resting outside in the tough-as-razors sea grass. The rain seldom stops falling on the Queen Charlotte Islands, soaking the soils and sea of those tiny green archipelagos on

BC's northern coast that are always shrouded in mist. The ground is soaked with grey fog, the main street of Queen Charlotte City a maze of cracks and potholes, all designed to catch and channel rain. Even the rivers on the Islands are continuously bursting their banks, their channels never quite sufficient to contain the rainfall. Once my father woke us up early, telling us fish were swimming in the streets, and we drove in morning wet darkness down logging roads held tightly by the branched hands of Alder trees, and we crossed tea-coloured streams and looked up to clouds filled with eagles ravens gulls screaming and fighting, and we turned the corner and there, swimming down the centre of logging roads, were fish by the hundreds, their stained and mottled spawning bodies ripping as they navigated the gravel and what little water was on the road. Streams had burst their banks, the rain was falling as always, and fish swam on roads.

In the eight years since I last lived here, nothing had changed. The docks still jutted out from the shoreline at ninety-degree angles, their bright red paint offering the only colour to a downtown core comprised of a legion hall, a grocery store, the only bank, a bar, and a combination hardware and apparel store. Here in this haphazard arrangement, all pieced together from metal siding, tin roofing, and plywood painted the same rust ochre as flats on low tide, is where I spent my junior high school years. It is where I walked long Friday nights, dreamt of running away, swore they'd always be my best friends, promised to keep secrets forever.

Now I was pulling in closer, working with Parks Canada doing biological surveys, still that sticky sweet sensation of escaping caught in the back of my throat as we came closer to the ragged shore, the edges of the town becoming clearer, the washed out fronts of houses near the ocean, grey from salt and wind beatings. Houses balanced on cliffs, it all still seems precarious—washed away and fragile. Red and yellow of the dock's water-beaded banisters, trawlers and seiners abreast three deep, seagulls screaming overhead, and the familiar smells of gas, tar, and fish; these remain all the same as well.

Eight years before, the longest years I had ever known, I'd left Queen Charlotte City on a ferry with my parents, destined for a small northern mainland community. It was as if the tide had gone out and for eight years had not come back in, that moment of my leaving etched in the exposed tide line, that point of departure as I watched from the back of that ferry as the islands faded into the black of ocean. Upon returning I am once again on the water, living for four months on a converted commercial fishing vessel, collecting invertebrates and streamside vegetation samples from Gwaii Haanas, the park on the southern tip of the Queen Charlotte Islands. We have caught walking Coho whose muscled fore fins allow them to scramble up rocks slick with algae; we have bottled skidding beetles, one living for two weeks in a vile of formaldehyde, no one can explain it, as if it simply shut itself down, swimming forever on just the surface. I have witnessed the shimmering blue of damsel flies colliding with mayflies breaking the surface of lakes innocent of glaciers, below the confused insects stickleback swimming, the males carefully tending their fish-built nests. For weeks as we witness these wonders, our supplies are flown in, and in all those months I saw only six other people, kayakers slipping through the cold waters near the shore, tourists enjoying the silence, never wanting to speak of such biological wonders.

As we inched around the breakwater, I caught the sounds of Queen Charlotte City. Dogs barking, lifting tones of voices independent of words. The trees on the shore, cars on the street, slowly came into focus through the clouds, and I looked at the tiny place I once knew as home. My clothes stank of kerosene from the stove on the boat; my rain gear was mud caked, and I had not showered for almost a month. In that haze of stench, each detail of this place that called me collides with me, reminding me of times past but dangerously near and close to the surface.

There is my house, balanced on the hill above the hospital, the hospital where I remember so clearly holding the hands of Charlotte, a Haida woman well over one hundred and three years old, her eyes milky with age, her teeth long forgotten, and her fingernails yellow and curling, this visit the idea of our school, that everyday one school-aged child should visit this Elder, and in hindsight I know how few schoolchildren must ever have had this chance, though at the time I worried the package of cigarettes in my bag might catch the notice of a passing nurse. There is the steep road leading to my house, and I am once again running down the pitted gravel past the salal bushes and salmonberry and devil's club and my father is angry above me, in this small town everyone is sure to know, voices echoing across the harbour and caught by cormorants resting on rocks fully dressed in gooseneck barnacles.

As I stepped off the fishing boat, my feet touching their first dock in months, the ropes made a high pitched squeal, and the boat whined as it rubbed against tires attached to the side of the dock, and I walked up the steep platform connecting the lower wharves to the top dock, made my way between parked cars. At the intersection of the dock and the main street was a sports tackle shop, hip waders and gaffs on display in the window, the roof lined with seagulls, new since I had lived there and invisible when we were pulling in. Beside this new business was something else I didn't remember. An old delivery truck, red paint applied broadly over rust spots, was pulled into the small gravel parking lot out front. A green piece of cloth stretched from the side door to two wooden stakes, everything flapping in the wind. A thin stream of water poured through a tear in the top. A table was set up under the wisp of cloth: peaches, pears, plums, and apples in mushy green cardboard boxes.

Faces are still familiar to me, just a little older but the same. I see the curly hair of a woman I went to school with, reminding me of those small classrooms, her eyes still behind the bright pink plastic frames of glasses that slip down her nose. Now, though, she has a small child in tow, and I am caught breathless that in this place of green rain and water she is now a mother, this girl, this woman, who sat with me in the belly of a yellow Grummon Goose plane, who watched with me the water rise over the windows as we moved off the landing dock and prepared to take off, restrained ourselves from grabbing each other's hands when the plane lifted out of the water, leaving a trail of water droplets against the sky, my mother waving at us from below, and we were winging through the sky to Rediscovery, a strange hybrid summer camp only conceivable on the Queen Charlotte Islands.

I remember it all so clearly, our plane landing in a bay near the camp, a canoe slipping through the ocean up to the belly of that yellow plane, she and I suddenly lugging our packs into the cedar stomach of a carefully carved craft. Ashore, we waited for the next plane filled with teenagers in an old longhouse on the beach, a longhouse used during sockeye season for fishing and smoking purposes, and inside the thick smell of smoke and cedar, the floor made of large pieces of stone. Diffuse light filtered in through leaves and needles covering a sheet of fiberglass used for the roof. We sat together, eating cookies and waiting in the house that was the centre of this village. We talked about who else we thought would arrive, about school and other friends. After an hour or so, one of the camp leaders came in and asked if we wanted to go for a walk and see one of the totem poles in the area. We all stashed our gear and made the twenty-minute trek over wet green moss and slippery seaweed-covered rocks to the Triple Watchman Pole. Three poles stood with their backs connecting, one looking over the ocean, one looking to the right, and one to the left. Great bear teeth and claws wrapped around the midsections, frogs hung out of the mouths of killer whales. On the top of each of the poles sat a watchman, a cedar hat on his head, his eyes open wide. The poles were now silvered cedar; pieces had been cut out, other sections had rotted. Salal and lichens grew around and on and around the poles, tree branches reached out and brushed at them, and the bottom of the poles were bones, now moss covered. The poles had been burial sites, there against the wind and waves bodies left for the elements, and my face turned skyward to those faces, and my friend of many years ago, now again so clear before me, leaned over to me and told me a story, a story about the carver of that pole, her great, great *chineye*, her grandfather Edenshaw.

Family is cut into the land in this city. We walked from one end of the town to the other, back and forth, back and forth, passing the docks and the community centre and the Federal Fisheries building Ministry of Environment Serge's gas station and taxi service fish and chip van techerages Kingdom Hall second hand store school Ministry of Forests and then the pavement ended, the other side of town, and you were through. How many cousins and aunts and second cousins did we meet on this stretch of road, how many things did we learn about each other following the line of the road from one end to the other?

From one friend I learned about death like no other death, death at the hands of someone you loved. Through the back alley, over the jutting piece of stone covered thickly in huckleberry bushes in the summer, down to the bend in the road by the lines of aspen trees, she met us with the news her stepmother didn't know she had left. The group of us picked our way down to a beach, rocks full of mussels and seaweed that is a thousand bubbles bursting under your feet crack crack as you walk, and I wanted to know all about her stepmother, the concept still foreign to me, something from Snow White and far away from this tiny town on the Pacific Ocean. Her answer still hums in my memory, goose bumps down my spine. It is not her stepmother she takes exception to, but rather that her father married so quickly after her mother's death. I recall being fascinated that a friend of mine, still so young, had lost her mother. Hungry for details I asked about the death, and there on a beach in Queen Charlotte City I learn of her mother's death. A loud weekend party, music spilling out over the ocean, the wind and confusion as her mother is accused of sleeping with her father's best friend and the two daughters following the screaming into their basement, still unfinished, sawdust on the floor and carpentry tools on benches and the table saw against plastic on pink insulation, and the screwdriver grabbed as an after thought by the best friend, stabbing it into the arms neck stomach of a mother. I will never see a screwdriver the same way again, referencing always in my mind that unfinished basement in Queen Charlotte City.

On the other end of town, Skidegate, a long walk, past the hotel the helicopter landing the boat launch the librarian's house with her pink Mary Kay car we laugh about at school past the doctor's house the ferry landing the museum the carver's shed the Chief's house and down to the cemetery on the edge of the reserve. For years this cemetery on one side and where pavement meets gravel on the other side brackets my entire frame of reference. I think often about all I know of the place between these two markers, of the pink house at the end of the driveway flanked by aspen trees, the only yellow gold during fall in Queen Charlotte City, Pacific Ocean city, rainforest city, city of green and grey. A huge family lives in that pink house, and I am always visiting, spending the night, escaping my own family, sitting in their living room with children grandchildren aunts uncles cousins steaming crab plates of smoked salmon jars of oolichan oil open to dip dried kelp with herring eggs. Here for the first time I swallow sea urchin eggs, slippery and orange down the back of my throat, I will myself not to gag, my eyes watering with the effort, I concentrate on the rustle of aspen leaves.

There is the turn in the highway outside Skidegate and near the museum. Here, black barnacled rocks slip into the sea, totem poles look to a horizon dotted with rounded green islands, and the small bay is clear water deep down to a small-pebbled bottom. This is the perfect place for grey whales, lolling within metres of the highway, infants nursing in the great salty cold waters, like a dream we are roaming, groups of bored teenagers standing on the road's shoulder witnessing this, the massive exhales of a whale's breath, tail, black side, tiny bright eye watching us watching them, they break the surface and gasp water, so close the breath of whales touches the highway we stand upon. I think back, remembering this from different vantage points in my life, and I know it to be magic. These whales have just swum from Mexico and beyond, their last pass moments ago alongside balancing rock, that oddity we have all tried to collapse, our backs against pockmarked black stone, as if we could push over what the tide that covered it each day could not. How strong and invincible we are in our own minds, strong enough to withstand the push of whales' breath, strong enough to pass unscathed through all this town threw at us.

I know in retrospect not everyone came through unharmed. Upon my return I meet the impossible, a woman living within the husk of a burned-out house—she, her brothers, and her son sleeping against walls now made of charcoal. Anything you touch here leaves a great gash of black stain. Because we once went to school together, she sees me when I step onto the dock and she invites me home with her; once there, we pick our way up a staircase in a house on the edge of town near where pavement meets gravel road and we sit at her kitchen table holding cups of steaming coffee and she tells me all that I have missed in the eight years since I left. She speaks of tragedy, of two twin brothers diving off a bridge, the stream below too shallow to break such a force, skulls meeting jagged rock beneath the surface. She speaks of joy with no boundary, of children being born and poles being raised and new teachers replacing old and swarming schools of silver salmon filling the nets of fisherman and the sightings of sea otters and whales and all that marks change and possibility for the future. Here again in this hometown of mine, my blood is charged once again. I am sitting in a house that stands in spite of being burned from the inside out, I am standing on land full with the impossible, and the water I drank years ago from the spring on the side of the road, kept parted by earthquakes, is suddenly at rest, a quieted compass needle knowing the direction of home.

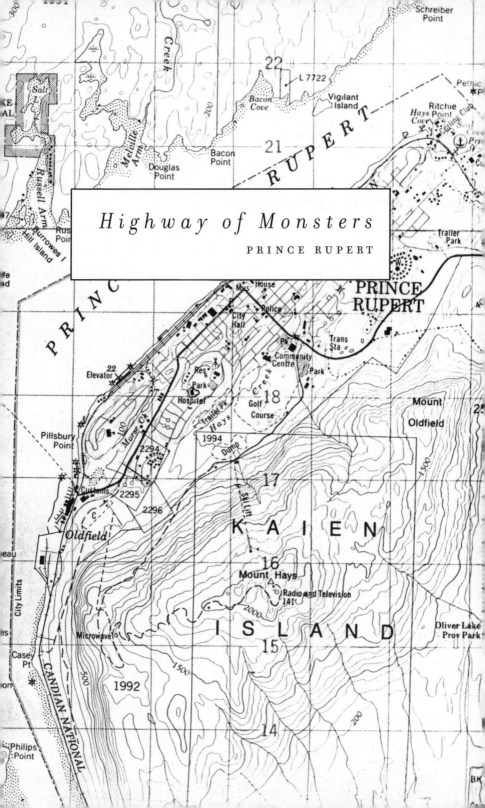

Highway of Monsters

PRINCE RUPERT

THIS JOURNEY TAKES PLACE ALONG A HIGHWAY flanked by monsters.

Where the road twists up and over Esker Bar, bordered by the blackened trunks of Cottonwood trees, Split Head Mountain rises against the horizon. Phosphorescent snow shining, skin against cloud, steam rising like hot breath from cirques. Edging pavement is the slippery river rising and falling, thick mud flats exposed, eel-grass wet and flattened. At low tide the waters of the Skeena, even a hundred kilometres upstream, are inhaled back to the ocean. Salt-textured ice blocks rise from the slick river bottom, great shards of tooth and bone opening themselves to the sky, seagulls circling, their voices slicing the wind.

People must be terrified.

It is the only explanation for Howitzer gun mounts found almost every fifty kilometres, for ridges of concrete barrier separating road from river, for the deep, half-cylindrical scars left from blasting caps detonated in rock faces.

Thin ribbon between Terrace and Prince Rupert, a stretch of road between forestry town and fishing town, between inland and coastal, between air full of Sitka spruce, hemlock, and then the smell of salal, muskeg bogs, and ocean. Fish, rotting nets, tar on docks, log barges.

Forgotten Prince Rupert, City of Rainbows. Oh yes, I know, all the locals say "city of rain." They say it knowing that once a family travelled down to Vancouver, children urging mother and father to

Science World and the unearthly white dome only possible in big cities, the docks and fishing boats of Prince Rupert so far away. The parents obliged, taking interest in a map of Canadian weather once there; when they located Prince Rupert, they pressed a button corresponding to rainfall, and from that map in Vancouver sprung a thin piece of metal, growing growing growing until it reached higher than any other city's thin piece of metal. The rainfall in Prince Rupert is unparalleled, but it does not drown monsters.

Did you hear about the family from South Africa? The one with children who were allergic to the sun, the family who came to Canada on visiting visas, knowing full well the visas would expire and they would face deportation. All this to live in Prince Rupert, city of rain, greyest community on the globe. If only Charles Hayes had not gone down with the Titanic. Great plans had been afoot, the possibility of the Grand Trunk Railway running straight to Prince Rupert. The port town would have burst the edges of its containing island, silver and gold would have docked morning noon and night, coal and lumber would have flowed directly across the Pacific. Prince Rupert would have been a city of prosperity, monsters put forever to rest. All this lost with the touch of a hull to an iceberg, the sinking of one boat and the drowning of one man, swallowed by a monstrous ocean.

Everyone dreams of what could have been. Prince Rupert, the Vancouver of the north, deepest port on the British Columbia coast. If only.

If only sawmills and pulp mills were not shutting down. If only Coho stocks were not depleted. If only Alaskan ferries had not been turned away. This depression is carefully guarded. Wouldn't want just anyone coming and going from Prince Rupert, a synaptical coil on the western tip of Highway 16, poised on hills, steep cliffs, and thin roads. The only way in by car, by rail, is cut with bridges, steel bangles on an arm reaching towards the coast. Travelling west and there is first the Exstew River, then the Exchamsiks River, and finally the Kasiks, all pouring green water into the fatty brown waters of the Skeena River.

Travel with me. Along Highway 16 and into Prince Rupert. In the spring. Here a cross, there a cross, old white paint, new plastic flowers, a symphony of tragedy, road accidents, trucking accidents, drownings, avalanche deaths. My mother's grade four class in 1995. A small desk empty, sickly loud, occupant killed with father driving home from a hockey game in Rupert. An evening chat, discussion about a paramedic friend. Did you hear? The highway's guy, the avalanche inspector. Killed the other day on the Rupert highway. Two crosses of many.

Between the bridges, on the bridges, around the bridges on the way to Prince Rupert.

Keep your eyes closed; the picture will become more focused. Be patient. A bald eagle, then two ten thirty fifty eagles, all along sandbars, on the ripped root systems of trees washed towards the ocean. The oolichan runs, tightly knotted islands of seagulls bent over silver schools, just below the surface. Black bears on railway trestles, avalanche tracks filling in with slide alder. It is spring in the story I am telling you, your eyes closed. A murmur of green has washed branch tips.

You are getting closer to Prince Rupert, hugging the narrow sides of Highway 16, you are passing the tight left hand turnoff to Port Edward, history of canneries, skeletal Skeena Cellulose, crab traps piled high, almost consuming a horizon of green islands in misty fiords. Now you can taste the salty air, the highway edged with red muskeg bogs, tiny contorted pine trees, and there . . . it seems absurd, but you simply turn a corner and after two hours of nothing but river trees mountains there appears a city, a high-rise hotel (the Highlander), brightly painted houses from the early years of the twentieth century, a time when fishing was good, when log booms were fat and thick on ocean waters, when cannery floors were slick with guts and the air seemed rich.

We have arrived. Follow my arm and look in the direction I am pointing. Do you see the bright blue hotel against the sky, cheerful dialogue with an imagined sunny sea? Re-adjust your vision and envision a bed thick with insects, tiny spots of blood from the bites of bed-bugs, coffee that tastes like insecticide, men working on fishing boats and falling exhausted, late at night, between sheets stained with the blood of other men. When they wake, their bodies full with an impossible need to scratch, they move to a different hotel—there, they move to the highest building in the city, twenty stories of concrete.

On the second night they awake from their beds in the tall hotel to the sounds of smashing windows, police sirens, and bullhorns. Look down from the hotel window, fourth story. Below, men are brawling on the streets, the bars have just let out, fights rupture on the streets, fights over fishing license allocation, over netting ground, over deckhands, wives, Federal Fisheries, stealing fish, over stealing space, getting cut out, over edging people out of prime water.

Desperation.

You can smell it on the pavement, the spot where one man has fallen, where another has connected boot to eye socket. The spot is reordered nowhere, it will disappear with the first downpour. No map, no survey, can capture it. It says this, though. People are afraid of a place like Prince Rupert, frightened to travel that highway of monsters, a landscape of gun mounts aimed at mountains. They do not want to be one more in a line up at the employment-counselling centre, in the UI office, in the grocery store buying on credit. At the bank to mortgage their home.

Follow my finger that way. A windowless building on the corner of Fourth Avenue, back alley against back wall, rusting green dumpsters behind. The employees inside have mounted a camera on their wall, to deter injectors from using the site. Inside are the home-support workers, the counsellors for anger management, family skills workers, and the community nurse who gives away free condoms.

These are the employed of Prince Rupert, the workers whose schedules are overbooked, their waiting room filled to capacity most days. They are paid to work with pain, employed to assist the broken hearted. Prince Rupert is overflowing, flooded, monsters everywhere. There is no shortage of work in this town for social workers and counsellors.

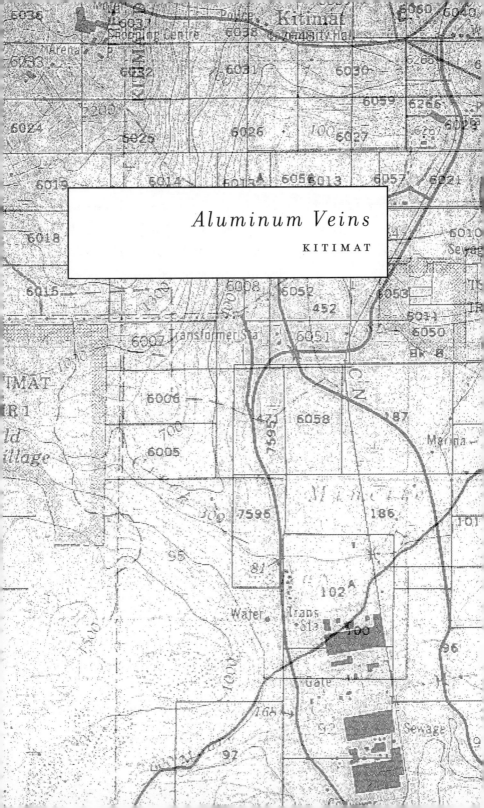

Aluminum Veins

KITIMAT

HOW FAR AWAY IS AWAY? HOW FAR AWAY IS FAR? FOR that matter, how far is far enough?

You want never to be seen in those places of your adolescence. The rust-bricked floor corridors of the Skeena Mall, the centre of it all, your mother's office in the back, around the corner, windowless and smelling faintly of the cleaning products used to sanitize the bathrooms in the town's only shopping centre. The cages behind the RCMP station, the kennels and grounds where your father trained dogs, where he met his second wife, eager to leave this dump, this no-action detachment, here only as a step to something better, somewhere else. The doctor's office where you went early in junior high, the first time you thought you were pregnant, and the doctor told you to abstain from sinning, to behave in a pure manner.

The pure of heart have nothing to hide, no need to run.

The steep corner around the bridge where your brother had his first and last car accident, where they pulled him from the wreck that was no longer even a vehicle and where you passed, over and over, vowing each time was your last, each time to move away. Far away. Far away from endless Friday nights of bootlegging booze from the manager of the restaurant where you worked, leaving after long shifts, hair thick with the fatty scent of cheese and pizza dough, cheap wine and parents who take their children to the one and only family restaurant, exhaling their cigarette smoke over their kids' heads and directly onto your green and white uniform.

Any goddamn place that isn't here, even if it's just over there, is far enough for you. It's away.

There. You have said it. Gotten it out. You hated it and you wanted to leave and you set upon a plan and you carried out that plan, and now you are here. Here in Kitimat and not in Terrace; not there, but away. It makes no difference that Terrace is less than an hour's drive from Kitimat. You think of all the land in between the two towns and you count your blessings, dreaming of the long winter days when snow makes the single connecting highway impassable. Your cheeks burn when people talk about how they do the short commute between the two towns in their pickups in the morning and then again each evening. Blood rushes to your cheeks when the distance between Kitimat and Terrace is made small, reduced in significance. You pre-fer to think the landscape impassable, certainly not navigable with mere trucks and engines. If only Kitimat and Terrace did not share an airport you could know people flew between the two towns. You could envision packing elaborate suitcases; luggage piled high, a safari jour-ney, something people may never return from. You want the distance to be dangerous, as dangerous as it is in your mind, your memories.

In your mind the terrain is a lifetime. Lakelse Lake, huge and deep, the Kitimat River, the chain of Onion Lakes, steep, rocky canyons and the uncharted territory of grizzly bears. For god's sake, one of the few triple homicides ever to have occurred in British Columbia happened in the endless space between Kitimat and Terrace, the as-of-yet unconvicted murderer vanishing without a trace into that vast, vast landscape between your old life and your new life. You married an Italian, someone from that tiny space of Europe that you have more than once run your finger across on a globe. He sympathizes with you, agreeing on the endlessness of the ninety or so kilometres between the two towns. Sometimes late at night you wake up shaking, sure you have not fled far enough—have not made a life you can yet call your own.

He holds you and together you stretch the landscape.

If this were Europe, you would be in another country, you would be of a different nationality, speak a different language, use a different currency. This is how far you have come, he assures you. You are separated by great distances from the town you grew up in, the town of your family.

You tell him about the rumours you heard at work, adding to the wondrous calming feeling of having escaped your hometown. At work a woman from the Haisla reserve outside of Kitimat is talking about a marriage: the marriage might be between a Nisga'a woman and a Haisla man, but joyous laughter is obscuring the details from what you are overhearing. An exchange of gifts is discussed, how the Haisla will give cockles and ocean gifts, how the Nisga'a will bequeath their legendary oolican. The Haisla's oolican is of course valuable, but since Alcan's aluminum smelter has reached mightily into the waters and mountainsides of Kitimat, locals say the fish taste like tinfoil. People joke that even the eagles have aluminum dreams.

This stretches the landscape, makes right your knowledge of great distances. These are two nations exchanging gifts from different worlds. They know the difference of currency, the difference of taste and language. You are mesmerized, happy to be held in the arms of your man from across the Atlantic Ocean, thinking of difference and distance, lulling yourself to sleep.

You do not ever complain about the factories and plants in Kitimat; never do you wish away Methanex, Eurocan, Alcan. Never do

you wish for the Kitimat River to not twist against smokestacks, produce Coho with heavy metal scales. You, for one, are happy about the
plants, have even been known to take night drives out to their wide
expanses of concrete, steel, and slowly blinking orange lights. Pulling
up along side Alcan's chain-link fence you think of science fiction
movies, stories of families sent to settle other planets, setting up great
factories to manufacture atmosphere. Thinking about being a settler
of another planet, the planet of Kitimat so far from your home, makes
you smile. You feel as though you have parked your car against the
massive, muscular flank of a giant monster; stock-still in your car you
convince yourself you can feel Alcan breathing, pulsating, aluminum
coursing through its immense factory veins. Your mind drifts from an
ever-present worry about being too close to Terrace. Instead, you
dream about a river diverted through the side of a mountain, an open
mouth of smashed teeth with water rushing through, damned and
cruel behind enormous turbines at Kemano, powering the economy
behind this town you call your new home. For a moment you think
about being transported, bodily, between places. You envision yourself as a salmon during one of the few labour strikes to have ever crip-
pled the dam at Kemano; an entire river shut down, water flow
reduced to a trickle as the sky reverberated with the silence of great
turbines shut down. Salmon by the thousands, twisting silver muscled
bodies grabbed by gloved hands and physically moved to another
stretch of water. A fish salvage project—you being salvaged from the
dried riverbeds of your hometown. An escape. It might be only one
watershed away, but the distance is a lifetime, and for a moment your
breath is deep and calm, listening to Alcan's heart pulsate, pumping
life through aluminum veins.

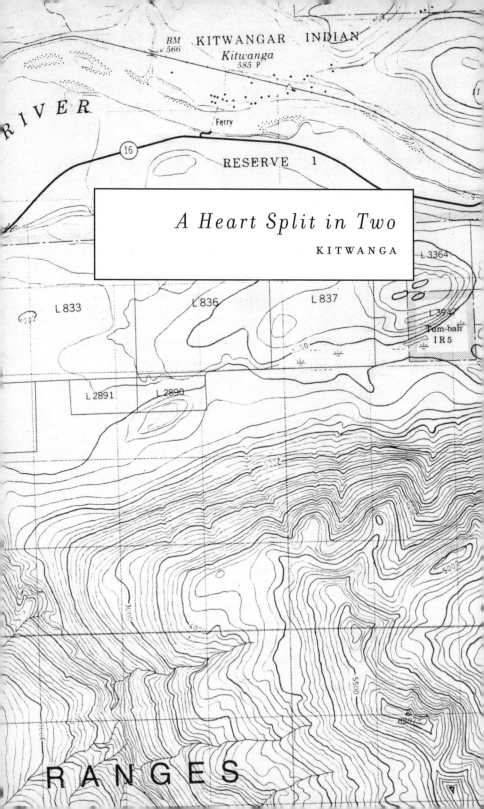

A Heart Split in Two

KITWANGA

THIS IS THE SITE OF YOUR FIRST HEARTBREAK. Split as easily as dry red cedar kindling, right down the middle. You can chart every road driveway front yard kitchen back bedroom backdoor side-yard, the neighbour's yard, the exact location of the truck and trailer, marked in memory. There. Beneath the rim where teachers, police officers, and clergy balanced themselves on high, is the reserve, Gitxsan schools, baseball fields, a stretch of totem poles against the Skeena River. There. Over the bridge and left from the gas station run by the Gitxsan Nation that sold ice-cream cones to summer tourists passing through enroute to Alaska. Or there, across the railway tracks that cracked open the road, split family from family when boxcars loaded with timber rushed through. These are the memories, the sites, mapped on your mind. A child's memory, perfectly clear. To this day, blood makes noise in your ears when you think of Kitwanga. To this day, your parent's divorce is a freight train splitting your heart in two, family from family.

At the age of seven you collected Christmas money, telling no one. Not in a tight-palmed sweaty bundle, or inside a hollow plastic animal, oh no, not you; you had a system as complex as the river networks around you. All pennies and nickels in envelopes cut in half, neatly retaped into pouches. Dimes and quarters deserved one whole-and-entire uncut envelope, just the corners reinforced with tape. And bills—these were stored with care in small folders hand-made of construction paper, the colour corresponding to the bill denomination. All this in your ten-year-old bedroom, a trailer still on blocks, a community of fewer than one thousand people stretching around you and great as the horizon of teeth-jagged mountains you only dreamt of climbing. For two years your money was carefully accounted for, filed neatly in a sequential way, and you limited yourself to one counting a month, though wherever you walked a careful tally followed closely behind.

The tally followed you past the husk of an old church, tall thin pillar of a wooden tower, whitewashed boards pulled off, ornate top almost Russian in style, stained glass windows clouded with the freezing thawing freezing thawing that marks this land. The tally followed you through railway tunnels and across rotting de-commissioned logging bridges, a cemetery overgrown with hemlock trees, cedar trees, weaving and clothing trees with scarred strips smooth and pulled from midsection to sky. You remember the edge of pavement and gravel, a marked irregularity for your wandering feet, from inconsistent smoothness to raw stone and gravel, a shift that marked your walk home from school each day, a mark among many. Out the front doors, past skirmishes and fights, you know of one that started when "fucking Nisga'a" was hurled from one Gitxsan boy to another, an insult ripping the scab from years of boundary and mountain range and carefully told zones around river edges and the thin tentacles of watersheds, an insult so local that to tell this story would confuse people even two valleys away. Here, in this locale though, it hurts with the pain of young men's broken faces.

Past this and across the railway tracks running parallel to the river, frozen almost entirely across from November to March, where there are sounds emitted like animals in heat as ice floe freezes on ice floe, as snow compacts river compacting snow against exposed shore and lichen encrusted rock. Across the railway tracks and alongside the local Kitwanga mill and logging business, the operator a small town hockey hero gone businessman, up to twenty trucks on his lot, owner of his own beehive burner, his own kiln, these are the sites of your carefully charted path home. The sweet blue smell of exhaust on mud on sawdust on diesel on metal and engine. Memories etched on your heart, broken in two. You knew that family well, the dad, the son, the mother and daughter, the richest family in town, always a new truck, more guns and rods than most knew how to count. They lived in a house down from yours. How could they not? In this town, everyone was down the road from everyone else. But here existed something else; they came over on Friday nights, formed a local band, the wife a drummer, your father the lead guitarist, your mother a singer. You heard the soft rifts of blues from behind the blanket that doubled as your bedroom door, and the tally in your head felt warm as if you held each bill beside your cheek, falling asleep.

The millyards led to the downtown, no more than a cluster of aluminum sided outbuildings; a Sears catalogue ordering counter, a truck stop diner, one other store you can't even remember the contents of, only that it sold everything from duct-tape to margarine, from tins of ravioli to used transmissions. And a lumberyard, you remember the lumberyard from the high clean smell of newly kilned two-by-fours in the rain. These small gestures to a core, a downtown, these are your endless wanderings, your hideaways and well-honed paths of walkie-talkie transmission, dreams of becoming an astronaut, even here outer space was alive and well.

The most amazing thing occurred over that Sears catalogue ordering counter. People talk about it, your family still laughs.

No one was there but you and the woman from down the road with the horses—she doubled on Wednesday and Friday afternoons as the Sears lady. You walked into the Sears building, all by yourself one month after your ninth birthday. You had that two years of Christmas money carefully itemized and filed in your coat pocket and the pages from the Christmas Wish Book catalogue carefully cut out, with the two items you'd wanted circled in black marker. The woman from down the road with the horses helped you fill out the order form, added the tax and let you count out that money, and three weeks and four days later she called you at home to let you know your digital watch and hot-rod car set had arrived. To your parents, it seemed like these items were delivered to you from the sky—it was an equally plausible explanation to that of a nine year old, without parents knowing, ordering items from the Sears catalogue.

Thinking back on it, you remember the whole great world being contained in that catalogue. It represented bright cities and wondrous possibilities that you saw reflected nowhere in your town of sawmill and gas station, one school and pitted baseball diamond. To your mind the Seven Sisters peaks, the red-purple runs of spawning sockeye salmon, even the day when you witnessed bald eagles tearing at a bear carcass— these were mundane in comparison to a city. These were not the events of news, of television or magazines. These were invisible but to the tiny populations who witnessed them first hand, who transformed the events to gossip and thus to forgettable items for an outside world.

When you were nine, even then, you yearned for the city. Just the idea of it. So you took it upon yourself to order in pieces of it.

The fragments of city did nothing to assuage the events conspiring to break your heart. Neither small town nor imaginary cities could do that.

Where did it start? You have tried for years to identify the elements of the disaster. You have never been successful, but through the process of re-visitation the incidents have become endlessly possible, each occurrence a possible starting point. Everyone in Kitwanga has a woodpile, cords carefully stacked along the sidewall, against the garage. Every house has a woodstove, and men lift heavy awls to split great rounds of hemlock or aspen. You are not sure if it was the first time, but you remember rounding the house and seeing your neighbour there, your mother's best friend, hand on your father's forearm. Then fights occurred, terrible rages that shook the trailer with wails and hollers you knew echoed across the valley, reverberating in the mountaintops. Your mother left, but she came back, and conversations stopped when you walked into school, all two hundred people knowing the exact happenings of your family. Was it before or after your mother left again that her best friend's husband kicked in your door? You are never quite sure, because at a point you are unable to articulate (again, you are not quite sure when) your heart simply broke in two. The smashing of your front door was followed by gunshots—these you remember only because of the magnitude of them. Then your father hauled you all into the pickup truck. This is clear because the truck was sold shortly thereafter—having been bought only because it was what everyone in Kitwanga drove. You know you left shortly after, but things remain complicated in your mind. You are not sure where you went to, only that leaving Kitwanga was leaving your mother. It was the last town of a whole family, and of one thing you are clear. The town was the site of your first heartbreak, a break as clean and complete as lightning splitting a silver cedar snag.

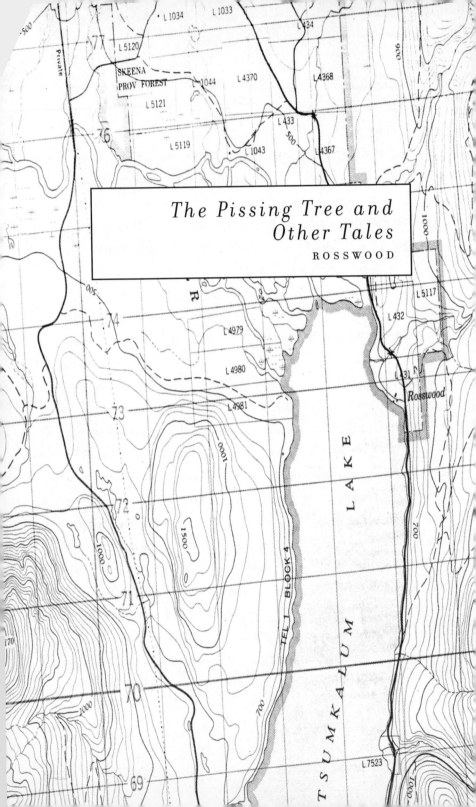

The Pissing Tree and Other Tales

ROSSWOOD

WHAT IS INVISIBLE REMAINS STRANGE. AND WHAT DID we know about magic? About myth and the impossible, about an excruciating life perched at the thin end of a lake, scattered through pine flats? In 1991, I fell in the shallow end of love, short lived and thin, with someone from Rosswood, hair thick and smelling like smoke, hands careful and blistered from working on engines, cutting firewood, and hauling water. This was magic, the magic of bees turning, turning, always facing toward home, an unknowable ability that those who produce the sweetness of honey have deep inside their tiny legs, deep inside their bodies so impossibly large for their wings. His family raised bees, hives of them in those Rosswood pine flats, and, invisible from most, that Rosswood boy let bees dance upon his hands, a dance of sunlight and a dance of facing home, always facing home, towards an invisible periphery containing his small Rosswood landscape.

The other side of this was sport. Difference was hunted, packs of hounds on strange scents, cornering and ripping. The school bus was a perfect hunting ground—disturbance amplified in such a small space, windows closed, air recycled through the heating vents. Stains that remained on shirts (no water), shoes too tight (your brother's and his brother's before that), dirt under nails, and the thick smell of pine smoke in hair (no power, woodstoves to keep warm). The Rosswood kids, the Rosswood families, those creatures everyone felt at liberty to hurt. Why not?

They lived so far out, on the outskirts, in the outback, far-away, in the middle of nowhere, at the ends of the earth, where no one would want to live anyway. Forty minutes drive on a twisting, slippery high-way, forty minutes outside our comfortable city of twelve thousand, our core, downtown, metropolitan centre, our urbaneness. Rosswood allowed Terrace to take its place as heart, as centre, as above and beyond the periphery. Rosswood was backward and violent, inbred and desperate.

What kind of mother named her daughter after the world's most famous woman pilot, dreaming a daughter soaring, a daughter impervious to pain? A daughter whose very name conjured heart and air. A Rosswood mother, hunted by her husband to the brittle door-ways of hotels and transition houses until the police gunned him down somewhere outside Atlin. Those are the kind of children we don't want at our Uplands school, up/lands, land of the upper, above the tracks, above the mills, up above highways and apartment com-plexes, certainly above (up up high high above) Rosswood kids. Those are children whose mothers simply say, "if that Terrace kid hurts you again, hurt them back, hurt them back more, and win," and with a name flying against uncharted horizons, a name that makes her pre-destined to soar, her feathers outstretched, she takes her Rosswood mother's words to heart, her fluttering and ascending heart.

Etched with the rigid handwriting of school principal, lips tight, three Rosswood kids suspended at once. They called out in painful hunted voices, voices from the edges of nothingness, and everyone turned away until the afternoon a Rosswood mother's advice came to haunt a school, daughters taking the son of a mill executive out across the mud-slick baseball diamond, across the soccer fields, and far away from the monkey bars and slides and swing sets and into the forest of low lodge pole pines encircling the school yard. They took that boy to the margins for which they had been mocked, the edges that made them always outsiders, always hunted, and in the long-light hours of early summer they hurt him back. Hurt him hard, holding him down, taking turns slamming rocks into him, cracking three ribs, one for each kid he had mocked, called dirty backward gross Rosswood.

You couldn't reason with families like that, children like that. They do not fit in. Not with the sons and daughters of mill executives, of company owners, of government workers, and shop managers. They could never share our schools, our clean and decent places.

They collected their water (drank it, bathed in it!) from the pissing tree. It's true, the pissing tree. Everyone knows about it, standing on the side of the highway, copper tube pouring eternal water pumped up from an underground aquifer. You could actually see them doing it, twenty-gallon containers in the beds of rusted-out pickup trucks, washing their faces, transporting it in bright red gas containers shining against fresh snow or long summer nights. Imagine. Water from a pissing tree.

No hydro until 1999, everything running on generators, driving through at night the air filled with a dull growl of Honda diesel generators, a perfect pitch with mating moose. Hand-built cabins, chinking still done with moss and mud, outbuildings built on outbuildings, you could even witness families chopping down pines, clearing and burning the land along the highway to put up fences, corrals for horses. You know how they run those generators? Oh, let me tell you. This is good, really good. Everyone knows about it, I mean you can hear it everywhere. All the contractors talk about it, it might as well be written in stone. Goes to show they're thieves.

They siphon it from logging equipment left overnight in

Rosswood. Get their hoses and gallon containers out and suck the fuel dry from those machines; sometimes graders, haulers, logging trucks are not even left with enough gas to start in the morning. A log hauler rendered useless for weeks on end, every night the gas tank emptied by Rosswood residents; over small hills they tromp, their packs of dogs chasing trucks down the highway, their gas cans and mason jars clanking in hand. We hear they sell it, and they probably do. Most of them never worked a day in their lives. Did you hear about that one guy? One of them . . . what was the family name again? Oh, you'd know if you heard it, that huge family—Smyths? Not that it matters—most of them are all related to each other out there anyhow. So, he was a brother, or cousin, or something, and he'd never worked a day in his life. But that's not where it ends, oh no. He wasn't even registered as being born. Had no Social Insurance Number, no birth certificate, no nothing. According to most of the world, he didn't even exist. Hands never touched cash. Did all his own hunting and trapping, traded stuff with other Rosswood residents, lived on moose meat and bears killed on the highway. Lived on road kill and water from the pissing tree. What more is there to say? He came into town on or about his thirtieth birthday. No one knows for sure because of course he didn't know his own date of birth. Came into town because someone figured out the government owed him back payments on the GST. Well, go figure—stealing gas for a living and now he feels he's got a right to back tax payments. That's what those backwoods people are like, balanced on the thin end of a lake, scattered over pine flats at the end of a thin, slippery section of highway.

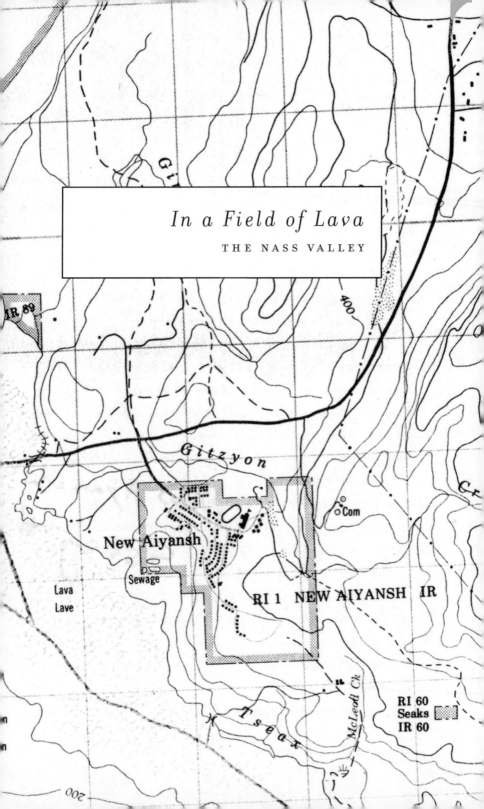

In a Field of Lava

THE NASS VALLEY

IR 89

Gitzyon

400

New Aiyansh

Com

Sewage

RI 1   NEW AIYANSH   IR

Lava
Lave

McLeod Ck

Tseax

RI 60
Seaks
IR 60

200

WHERE THE LAVA STOPS, THE THIN, SWINGING SUS-pension bridge begins.

Gitwinksihlkw seems to be situated where the lava flows end. The bubble of grey rock falls into the Nass River's green-brown waters as they boil through the narrow canyon that separates the gravel parking lot from the tiny village.

The bridge between Gitwinksihlkw and the parking lot sways with the wind, it shudders and resists as you walk across it. It is only three feet wide—just barely space for two people to walk abreast. A strange sensation can be felt when walking over this bridge. The wind rushes over you and the bridge, the waters below seem still against the movement. For a few moments you are truly suspended. Looking down between spaces in the boards, the grey waters of the Nass River seem oddly close though they are over thirty feet below the bridge.

In times of flood, when ice in the headwaters starts to melt, the water has been known to pour over the bridge, consuming it.

Until 1998, no roads entered the village of Gitwinksihlkw, and the tiny community comprised only a few houses. Some of the house windows were broken, doors on the second story of other houses lead into empty space, testimonies of balconies that had long ago fallen off. People, still to this day and even with the advent of roads, back their trucks filled with groceries into the parking lot carved from lava, unload their supplies into wheelbarrows, and cart them across the bridge into the village.

In the summer of 1992, I came here to cook in a logging camp just outside the village of Gitwinksihlkw, where the lava fields come upon you suddenly, as if you have turned a single corner and suddenly entered another dimension.

The road I came in on winds into Gitwinksihlkw along side Lava Lake, water striking blue green in the summer sun, even more brilliant clustered as it is in the grey lava rock. Local legends have it that cars have twisted off the thin road into this lake. People in the Nass Valley say it's the deepest lake in BC, telling stories over and over again of the logger who remains death gripped to the wheel of his rig, stuck deep and never recovered from the bottom of this lake.

Locals warn their children about the day when the logger will surface.

During the summer, against the lakes and rivers, the lava becomes a problem for fire fighters. Rock moulded from fire, it holds fire well. Sparks get caught in small but deep crevices in isolated corners of the lava fields. There they sit, smouldering for days, the thin line of smoke disguised by dust blowing over empty rock.

Fire travels through lava like blood through veins.

It finds intricate arterioles and tiny paths, and through these thin spaces moves great distances. When you are least expecting it, in the least likely place, the fire jumps from the lava and ignites everything in its path. There is no way to see it coming. You must wait for its arrival, hoping it won't spring up near a dry stand of timber, or worse, too near to a village.

Summer in Gitwinksihlkw brings the sockeye running up the Nass, to the edge of the lava and under the bridge between parking lot and village. A huge fish wheel, slowly turning in the water, plucking fish up and lifting them live to people who sit grabbing the ones that are big enough, throwing ones that are too young back. Lines of red fish flesh stretch across the village, children run around with pieces in their mouths, the smell of smoke everywhere. Women fillet the sockeye on huge pieces of plywood, holding the fish by its tail and sliding a knife between the silver skin and the red meat. Guts and heads of fish slick the paths in the village, and seagulls scream overhead by the thousands.

Long ago people of the valley lived in a large village, the largest one in the Nass Valley. According to legend, children from the village went out to play with the fish in the river one day, though the chiefs had warned them against this. Again the chiefs warned them not to, and again the children went out and played with the fish. One night, after repeated warnings, the children once again tore bark off trees, rolled it up, and, setting fire to it, they stuck it into the backs of the fish. The fish looked like boats with lights swimming in the water. Suddenly, the children heard a great rumble in the upper part of the valley, and they saw the lava rock pouring their way. Their games with the lit bark in the backs of the fish caused lava to flood the valley, and forever more the tiny communities seemed to exist in the midst of emptiness, of sky, mountain, and lava.

There are no food stores, no clothing stores or restaurants or banks in Gitwinksihlkw. The local hospital, down the road and to the right and then up again through a new arm of lava, is small. No overnight stays are allowed unless the weather has taken out a road, and when the roads are all right to drive, the New Ayainsh ambulance can make it to Terrace, the closest community of any size, in two hours. I'm told that, having no other options, sometimes people have to will their appendixes not to rupture for a couple of hours.

I came to cook in Nass Camp, a logging camp also at the edge of the lava. My summer is bent over steel stoves and greasy food, feeding loggers and fallers three times a day and sharing small aluminum bunkhouses with them at night.

I am here because I need the money.

In the evenings I have been bitten by mosquitoes, I am exhausted from peeling potatoes, feeding fallers. My back is sore, and I walk outside in the late-night summer sun through skeletons of heavy-duty machinery that dot the gravel lot. Rusted yellow mouths of graders, forgotten flat beds of eighteen-wheelers resting on their sides and disintegrating in the rain, the odd box of an old gravel truck.

Dusk turns the skylight purple, flocks of ravens cry overhead, black specks against the horizon, they fly to unknown destinations. At night black bears roam the perimeters of the camp, their snuffling pig-like sounds clear through the thin windows of my bedroom.

During the hours I have off in the middle of the day, I sometimes make the short drive to the logging camp's dump, a levelled-off piece of land always smoking against the sky, a high and rotting smell greeting me, the taste of burnt plastic in the back of my mouth. I make this drive to watch the grizzly bears, huge and strange amongst heaps of garbage. Often a mother grizzly has two or three cubs with her following along behind her, tearing at black garbage bags, cans like peanuts in their mouths. If you go through the garbage a grizzly has scavenged, you find cans that look like they have been target practice for a kid with a pellet gun. The bears put the entire can in their mouth, run their tongues around the inside, chew it some more, and then spit it out. Like someone eating sunflower seeds.

Even in this burnt land of garbage, their power is unmistakable.

I am trained to cook for men who work in the bush. I am trained to make more food than I thought it possible to consume.

My teacher, Glen, was not a tall man, but rather thick and broad like a pit bull, priding himself on being the best logging camp cook in the Northwest. Travelled up from his native California at the age of twenty with a chef certificate in one hand and a dream to own land in the north. He worked for offshore drilling companies, mines in the middle of nowhere, and now as head cook in Nass Camp. He always wore a formal white chef uniform, complete with hat. Glen had blue eyes, a shock of almost white blond hair to match his white hat. He had hands that could grab a bread pan straight out of the oven, no mitts needed.

For several weeks I dreamed of those hands, dreamed of them on lava as I braided together people and landscape, logging camp and villages.

The first time I met Glen's wife, I was hauling Glen out of the small bar behind the kitchen. He was yelling at fallers, screaming he'd piss in their food for a month, don't think he wouldn't. I had him under the arms, pulling him, and he was trying to walk backwards, stumbling.

At first, I could not get over how hugely pregnant this woman was, back arched with the effort of walking upright, holding her head back, belly thrust forward. Then I could not get over her strength, the way she seemed to lift her husband effortlessly, talking to me all the time, explaining he does this from time to time. Ties one on. How she will bring him back to her village, how her relatives will help her pack him over the bridge, help her lift him into bed, and, finally, help her settle her own huge and pregnant self into bed.

Even to this day, I am not sure I ever got her name. As time went by, and we spent more and more time together, it seemed impossible to ask, like admitting a sin. Then it seemed the opportunity just did not come up. Strange to think I can only refer to her as *Glen's wife*, as *she*.

As the summer moved on, she came to visit me more and more, working around the kitchen. Kitchens in logging camps are some of the most beautiful kitchens in the world. Solid stainless steel, grills the size of small banquet tables, vacuum-sealing ovens that can roast half a cow at one time. Logging camp kitchens are built to cook for the appetites of loggers, built to accommodate the needs of giant stomachs. When you peel potatoes for dinner in a logging camp, you peel twenty-five pounds of potatoes, and they're all gone by the end of a meal.

She made salad, standing over the sink, her huge swollen belly stopping her from getting too close, washing each leaf with a careful precision. She and Glen would talk about the baby, about the work they were doing on their house, about her family. Her little sister graduated that summer, she told me. It had taken four attempts, but there was another high school diploma in the family. The graduating class that year in New Aiyansh was seven people, three of whom had kids. The logging camp catered the celebration; I served little white buns and cold cuts, slices of cheddar cheese and tiny pickled onions, to hundreds of valley residents, all out for the community celebration. It was like nothing I had ever known. People from up and down the coast came, crowding into the school gym and dressed in satin dresses and tuxedos, button blankets and cedar skirts.

Outside, the doors of the school opened under the beaks and

mouths of huge creatures, ravens and frogs, their eyes looking across the lava beds of the Nass Valley.

Her water broke late that night. I was told this the next morning, small parties visiting the kitchen, bringing the latest from Gitwinksihlkw, cars of grandparents, babies, and teenagers making the drive to spread the news.

The newest baby of the Nass Valley was named for the lake he was born beside.

In a small house in Gitwinksihlkw, her contractions started. She sat up for quite a while, in that strange state I'm told you enter before giving birth. She wasn't sure whether or not to get Glen out of bed, but finally, when the contractions were so close together she could no longer handle the pain, she woke Glen. Again, as I'm told some men do, he entered a strange state of panic, grabbing the "birth bag" they had ready by the door, supporting her across the suspension bridge, and into their car. Then they decided they could make the drive to the hospital faster than the ambulance, and Glen's wife assured him she could hold on for just a little while longer.

Lines of grandmothers telling me the news said Glen drove the steep and twisting roads out of the Nass Valley as fast as he could, sped around the switchbacks beside Lava Lake, and made the paved section of highway in record time. They were forty minutes outside Terrace's hospital when Jen's water broke. They parked beside a long thin northern lake, barren faces of alpine mountain slopes encircling the highway, the car, the two parents. She moved into the back seat and once again Glen panicked, I'm told. But his wife became perfectly calm, knowing exactly what to do. She gave birth to a perfectly healthy boy beside a lake, under the faint light of an early morning northern summer sky, mountains filling the horizon. Together they drove into Terrace with a little boy in their arms, met doctors at the doors of the emergency room, doctors who had nothing left to do but congratulate new parents.

My summer in the lava bed ended the day after the newest baby in Nass Valley was brought home to his village. A mother's face, a tiny little boy in her arms, in front of a window overlooking the lava beds. I wasn't sure I would ever return to the Nass Valley, and it was this face I took away with me, leaving on the same road I came in on, passing the place on the side of a highway near a lake where a child had been born in the back seat of a car.

Years later, I made the journey once more. In the winter. I made it two days after I had done a routine visit to the transition home in Terrace, that community where so many summers ago Glen and his wife had walked into the nearest hospital, baby in arms.

I was working in the community's women's centre and a woman I was working with was staying in the local transition home. November is a cold month in the north, filled with grey and sleet, the wind never ending, the horizon always close and claustrophobic with clouds. Walking down the hall of the transition home, I bumped up against a young boy running out of one of the bedrooms. I stopped, bent down, and went with him into the room he had just come out of.

The face of the woman in the bed was the face of so many women in transition homes. Eyes thin swollen lines in purple blackness. Lips cracked, dried blood against two broken front teeth. Her hand reached from under the covers to take hold of her son, and I still did not know her name, though her son's name did not need to be spoken.

The name of a lake, a lake he was born beside. A northern lake between a village in the lava beds and small town hospital.

I made the journey in the wintertime only to remind myself of a place that I had left and that I had not returned to. On this trip, there was no greenness of lava lakes under sunshine, no fields in bloom with cottonwood pollen filling the air. Instead, the lava fields were smooth under metres of snow and ice. The sky was bigger than I recalled, no leaves on branches to block anything out, the mountains like cut-outs against a steel winter sky.

The bridge to Gitwinksihlkw was slick in a thick encasement of ice. The huge cables anchoring it to the sides of the Nass River canyon were smooth, the ramps on either side of the bridge danger-ously slippery. Two children from the village were hauling a bright purple plastic sled from one end of the bridge to the other. They were taking turns riding in it, building up speed as they ran across the bridge, hurtling themselves over the icy ramps. Below them, chunks of ice the size of houses broke up in the river, bashing together and sending spray up to the cables and mesh, adding another thin layer of ice to the bridge.

As I made my way over the suspension bridge into Gitwinksihlkw, I noticed for the first time the small white church about twenty-five metres down stream. Once I had crossed the bridge, both feet now in Gitwinksihlkw and the snow-covered flat-ness of the lava across the river now, I picked my way along the icy path to the building. In the strange grey light that takes over the Nass Valley in the winter, the church seemed even more run down than it truly was. In fading red letters above the doorway, which was now boarded and sagging, was the emblem of the Salvation Army.

The windows of the church were smashed and gaping open, the

entire structure leaning into the wind. It seemed like at any moment it would fall into the waters of the Nass River and be washed away forever. I bent down into the snow to look at the old building from the bottom. It was only from this angle I noticed the church's foundations.

At first, as breath steamed in front of my eyes, I thought I must be mistaken.

But as I bent lower, my hands freezing against the snow, eyes of bears and killer whales could still be made out. The huge logs making up the foundation were totem poles, hacked and sawed so the church could be built on top of them, slowly turning to earth in this tiny village on the edge of the lava.

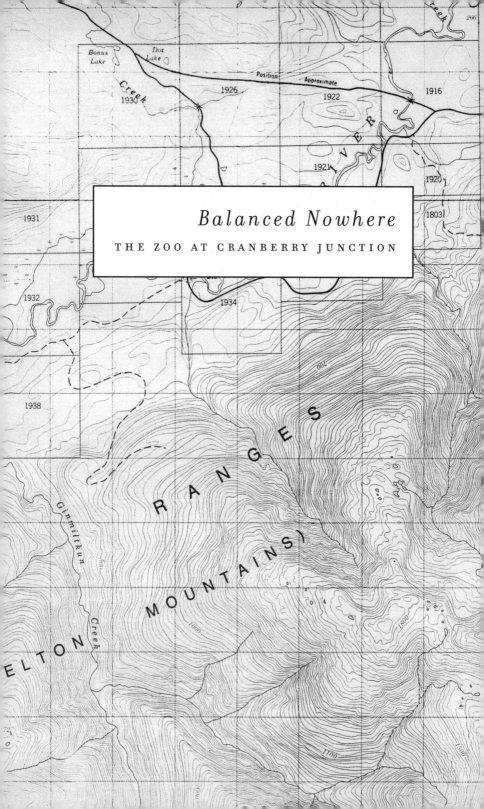

Balanced Nowhere

THE ZOO AT CRANBERRY JUNCTION

THE SMELL OF SMOKE REACHES YOU FROM OVER A mile away, high and floating, a messenger of population in a landscape of emptiness. Compared to anywhere, this is nowhere, and against the grey and clouded sky a dull orange glow is the only thing lighting the horizon. The tent city comes into view slowly, disappearing as the road curves, appearing again, splintered between the wind-blown and upturned sliver cottonwood leaves, broken up for a moment through the whiteness of aspen trunks.

It is a colourful and pieced-together place, rusted red trucks against yellow converted school buses, tents and tarps, trailers and rough-plank shanties. From the road it is impossible to imagine the spread of this small and seasonal city, impossible to judge the intricate and interwoven lives and stories taking place inside each dwelling. At peak season, this place, the place everyone calls "The Zoo," bursts to capacity, filling like a stream in spring runoff. The Zoo can claim over three hundred inhabitants; travellers, tourists, campers, modern nomads, mushroom pickers, all balanced on the edge of nothing, balanced nowhere.

What do you notice first as you swing off the highway, the shocks of your car tested as you careen through gaping potholes, the air thick with smoke, in front of you behind you all around you, the bloated frames of canvas tents saturated by rain? You notice the carefully constructed plywood frame of a cooking hut, the warm smell of deep frying competing with campfires, the sound of sizzling somehow out of place in the landscape of flat tundra and pine trees. Enter the cooking shack, its windows made of opaque plastic flapping where staples have ripped loose in the seaming, and you enter the world of an eating and gathering building, the world of Geraldine and Zenon (in this story of remoteness, who could imagine better names than these?). These two, this seemingly ancient couple, tell their stories while slowly drying huge gray plastic tubs used for storing potatoes; they tell their stories while sitting, while lighting cigarettes with the matching hands of old people who have known so much time and so many places together, hands with the texture of rainforest blow down, so many lines overlapping.

They come all the way from Quebec, come up every summer as the months of June and July spread their long days across the north, saying they get mostly pickers, some fishermen and tourists, some nice folks and some not-so-nice ones, all travelling the grey lines of highways that lead toward Alaska. For four years they have made this journey north to a cluster of tents and tarps, thinking about all they have known, all they have seen, the people living in the backs of their trucks, the people with torn, wet tents and children balanced on their backs, the people that are not even living, just existing from place to place to place, the road long, uneven, and hard.

Inside the cookhouse, slowly filling with blue fingers of cigarette smoke, pickers begin to enter, mushroom pickers with their white plastic buckets in hand, their thick wool pants and muddy hiking boots, banging off sand and the deep rust red soil made up of rotting wood and coniferous needles. These people who move with such direction in the woods, these people who are lost upon the rest of the world as all nomads are, enter the warm plank and plastic kitchen, pulling up chairs to rough tables covered with red and white synthetic sheets, and the air quickly saturates with blue smoke, the smell of deep frying and grill cooking.

Two young people come in with the requisite bang of a screen door on uneven hinges closing behind them, one tall with the frame of a man comfortable in himself and comfortable with the land around him, one small and bright with long hair and a body with such natural beauty that even the limp grey Stanfield sweater she wears cannot hide it. When one searches for stories about the tent city, these are the two people with whom to speak, stories about everything resting but a breath from expression. They met in this microcosmic metropolis; fell in love with each other and the land and the life of mushroom pickers. Fell in love, perhaps, as anyone might, gazing at stars or walking the back streets, and every year they come back to this tiny tent city, driving Highway 16 west all the way from Prince George.

His story is this. There is what he calls a draw; a pull strong and urgent, a certainty that you can be in the outdoors and make a few bucks, a possibility he describes as a nice marriage, a union of sorts, for those not able to be conventional. The Zoo is large for a tent city, but it is certainly not alone. Each year, seasonal cities appear around northern British Columbia, off logging roads, tucked into the mid-river islands of the Skeena, clustered in forest clearings. One island in the Skeena River draws anglers to a Lazy Boy chair propped on a sandbar. Another of these northern tent cities is but a collection of tents that circle the back of a local restaurant in Terrace. In others, vans, buses, and tents are found parked in tiny communities on the logging roads west of the city. There is something unique about the people who live in these cities, far from the running water and cinder block mini-malls of most northern British Columbian towns, these people seem to have a touch of the nomad running through their veins, a hint of modern-day Gypsy in the blood, and this is what the story tellers speak of, equating themselves to beaten dogs, the images of animals running from some unspecified thing, some impossibly unknown that is so awfully clear for those running away from it. These are people who say they have been hurt, never more specific, shy always of the detail, comfortable with the general. In that generalness of hurt they gather among the summer nights in the rusted frames of gutted vans and the thin frames of nylon or acrylic tents. They search always for the bright white tight balls of pine mushrooms and then, later, when the leaves have begun to fall, for the fat orange bodies of Chantrelle mushrooms, money in moss, profit from the forest soil.

The people who live in, or move through tent cities, are people who, according to the stories told, are people seeking to live just a little outside the rules of regular society. They are people attracted to the lifestyles only frontier living can offer, and it is a mystery even for those who live the life, for those who try to explain it to an outsider like me. But there are things universal, even amongst these northern nomads in The Zoo and the tiny paths and rutted makeshift roads and handmade dams in the small creek that provides water: everything pulses with complexities as intricate as any urban centre. There are main streets and politicians, a tiny collection of trailers the locals call China Town, brightly coloured plastic mats outside the doors, plastic slippers and flip-flops lined up at the doorframes. The Zoo even has a local preacher, a man with suspenders and not a day of formal training in his life, his tent filled with scripture duct taped to the walls, his job to place readings about god in all the local outhouses, his face open as the great sky above and his stories about all the confessions and sins, each of which he takes to heart, each of which he believes he can solve.

The gravel "Main Drag" of The Zoo edges everything from the cookhouse to a tepee, and thins slowly out at the north end of town where the potholes get deep and mean, filled with grey water. Walking around them is difficult navigation, and by this time people have come to watch you, wanting each and everyone to tell you their own stories of this tent city, of their lives of wandering, and by way of introduction they shake their heads and apologize for the potholes, as if some failure in municipal government has caused them, as if these streets could be any other way. One person justifies the gaping divots in the hard-packed gravel road, saying they are the local's version of speed bumps, that without them people would fly through the tent city, mindless of basic considerations. So these potholes are transformed into bylaws, a nomad's law.

From these conversations of potholes I am taken to an area where the sky is obscured with tarps, blue and orange, stretched and overlapping in a jig-sawed roof, patched with green garbage bags, the rain kept carefully at bay so locals can gather around fires burning in oil drums, woodstoves constructed carefully from the gas tanks of great eighteen-wheel rigs, chimneys careening through the tarps up and away to the stars. Here sit Pearl and George, folded into plastic lawn chairs, their faces lined and their hair yellowed from smoke, and I learn that George is the mayor of The Zoo, and everyone laughs and I shake the calloused hand of George while Pearl pulls her sweater a little tighter across herself and the wind picks up, the tarps shaking as if with laughter as well. Talk turns to the truckers who gossip about The Zoo on their radios, and another log is added to the belly of a woodstove, and then the small group we have acquired takes me deeper into this tent city, the road getting thinner and thinner, the cottonwood trees along the edges getting thicker. From the end of the road come children's laughter, louder than the rustle of leaves, and then, around a bend, appears a small trailer, the kind you drag behind a car, and it looks out on a yard of firewood, beaten-up water containers, frying pans, assorted food cans, and a bright red trike. Almost hidden in the trees behind the house, four boys are jumping high on a slightly rusted trampoline, yet another tarp, the millionth use of a tarp in the city held together by them, and the boys are yelling and laughing with their faces turned skyward. As we walk by they stop their great skyward propellings, showing us a raven they have penned, saying the bird is unable to fly, and removing him from the cage they hold him in their carefully cupped hands as they begin again to jump, the bird's heart soaring, I am sure, each time bodies leave the ground, and the boys call to our backs that the raven, bird of myth and bird of wonder, loves to eat potato chips.

Reaching the outer edge of The Zoo is where the stories reach their limits, and for brief seconds the hurt and running that defines these people is brought to the surface, stories of deep sadness and people who drink before they eat, women who arrive with bodies torn from truck drivers who exchange sex for mileage, families with nothing who arrive here thinking they can pick money from the forest floor, thinking that mushroom picking is easy, not knowing that it breaks the bodies of those who too often have broken spirits. There are stories of a woman from Vietnam who came across Canada from Thunder Bay, Ontario, arriving without even a bucket or boots, who believed myths she had read in Canadian Geographic about a forest floor paved with gold. Had her character not been broken before she arrived at The Zoo, people said, both her body and spirit were destroyed in the journeying. The numbers speak for themselves: of the one hundred and twenty-five residents of The Zoo last year, three were already dead. Many more were simply lost, unheard of and unheard from.

There is laughter though, laughter among couples in love, happiness for a moment touching, intertwining, but then breaking as the night is again ruptured with cynicism, and the stories turn to other pickers who follow each other to carefully guarded mushroom patches in the forest, of people stealing firewood and money from fellow tent city citizens, about garbage left in the forest, wilderness forever marred by the hands of those who seek it, work it. As light begins to fade against the broken-down and broken-in colours of The Zoo, the wind picks up and tarps rustle and tents sway and lamps start to blink out inside the houses of this tiny tent city, and Geraldine Normand, back in her plywood cookhouse, offers a final piece of wisdom about the wandering and sometimes-lost people who show up in her kitchen, saying that in all the years she has come to The Zoo, she does not have many complaints—the people, like all people, are nice to you if you are kind to them, that if you feed them well, their hearts are calm for a moment on the edge of this great wilderness.

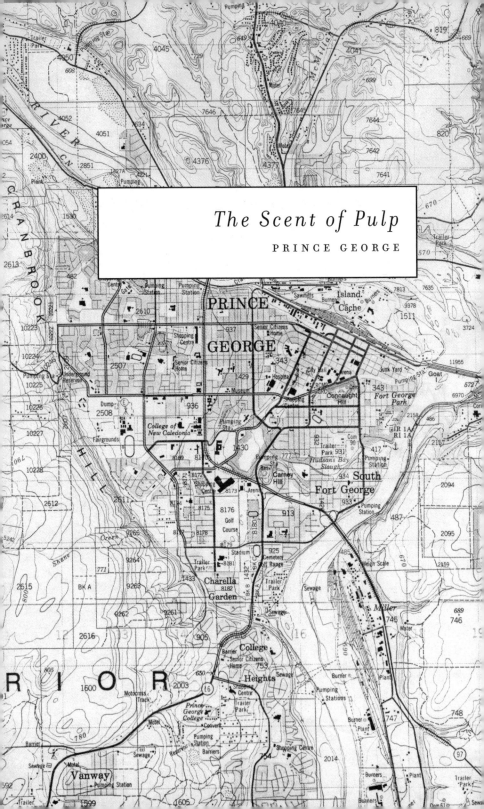

The Scent of Pulp

PRINCE GEORGE

WHAT ARE MY MEMORIES OF THIS TOWN, LIVED IN SO
fleetingly, yet such an impact made?

It seems in memory to always be seen from above.

I am flying into it, returning from the so many flights we all make
out of it, out to Vancouver, out to Victoria, out to Toronto Ottawa
Winnipeg Saskatoon Montreal. There are so many places to fly away
to; we become community in the sky. We people from Prince George
know each other well, strengthening our ties in the airport, our gates
always the same, our complaints etched into the walls. We are
patient. Patient through the snowstorms that delay our return to
family, patient through the planes that are always late to arrive, even
later to leave. When unexpected layovers imprison us in the big cities
of the south, we share our hotel rooms, worried about what might
become of our fellow northerners, content to sleep across from
strangers but for a similar landscape. After all, in order to leave we
have all left our houses before five in the morning, a requisite of flying away and onto somewhere else, somewhere known. In late
autumn the sun rises as our wingtips touch the sky, the horizon a thin
line of orange and red against grey-silver night cloud. Every time I
leave, I look to the sky and think of salmon my father has caught and
cleaned, the belly sliced open from tail to gill, a thin blood line surrounded by milky grey and silver scales, a northern sunrise.

Or I am looking down on it from the lip of a cut bank, ancient lake
shore now sculpted by the Nachako meeting the Fraser River, both
also leaving Prince George, destined for the softened, cultivated lands

of White Rock and Delta, then out into the ocean, waters used as port in Vancouver. Viewed from above it is an archaeological find: dainty brushes have dusted out streets filled for centuries with sand and ancient lake silt, trained hands have swept around the buildings, this maze, this fossil-like lace, this city in a bowl that is not a real city. Even the rivers rush southward in their search for true cityscapes. From the vantage point of this cut bank, Prince George is but a burst of small light, a meeting place of railway track river road five perhaps six tall buildings scattered suburbs factories bridges and mall. It is surrounded on all sides by forest bog lake spruce pine muskeg moose bear oceans of cattail and salmon berry. This is what wins in the battle of abundance. The city is small in a landscape of wilderness; it is even smaller when viewed from above. Enter from the west and you enter from above, coming down, down into Prince George, the road full of loaded logging trucks, the hill endless with the scent of burning break pads. Enter from the east and you must also come down down, this time over the great arms of the bridge that stretches from one bank of the Fraser River to the other, all along your right hand side the landscape of pulp mills and then a prison that overlooks them, directly in the wind path of great clouds that billow forth from the smoke stacks, the stink of pulp meeting the faces of prisoners.

I arrived in late summer, a Williams moving truck following us from Terrace, leaves turning blood red along the banks of the Skeena, the Bulkley, and now into this watershed, so new altogether, the conflux of the Nechako and the Fraser, a city resting as if excavated from sand, a city contained by cut banks and moraine hills. I do not yet know this, but the bowl is two palms pressed together, holding in the breath of Prince George sky.

I will find out, as winter dawns, the days shortened, the world colder than anything I have previously experienced, anywhere I have ever lived. No one told me about great gulps of frozen air, your lungs with a stuck feeling, constricted. I will find out; that we have moved from 650 kilometres west of Prince George, where we lived and worked for the previous three years, that we moved to coldness like nothing else. Procuring the moving truck has been a feat in itself. With people fleeing the north, with population decreases and every morning the news of rips in our economic fabric, moving trucks are difficult to find. They come into town at a much lesser rate than they leave—and virtually as quickly as they arrived, families leaving the region claim them. Everyone seems to always be leaving.

In the end, we are successful in hiring a truck only because the wife of our landlord worked for the Williams moving company, and the company manager agreed to save us space at the back of a container already booked by another family. We have four hours to unload all our possessions in Prince George before the moving truck thunders on across the Alberta border and into Edmonton with the original family's belongings.

Our rented Prince George house is located on a small side street and within walking distance of the city's downtown core, situated within distance of all the amenities in a northern capital town, and in this city, this not quite a true city but not really a small town like so many other places we have lived, we are situated behind the Sikh Temple. At night, from our kitchen window, we can see the great flagpole at the temple's front light up and shine its methodical blue flashes, created lightening in blackness or against snow.

We are one of the few houses in front of which a pickup truck is not parked, because here trucks are tools, bashed in and dirty, puffing blue exhaust, small wives drive their husbands, 4 x 4s to the mall, chat before churches in trucks they need to swing into like construction workers climbing scaffolding against skyscrapers. Here trucks are skyscrapers, the city sky scraped with them, hauling, moving away. We are located on the northern end of our street, and as with many other north–south running streets near Prince George's downtown, ours ends in an embankment leading first down to the railway tracks and then to the Nachako River. In the evening, the sun sets against the cut banks, and throughout the day, and often throughout the night, great trains of one hundred cars or more, loaded with lumber or pulping chips, rumble along the tracks heading west towards the coast from the city's five mills, the great gasping mills that heave blue smoke into our air.

I imagine being that smoke, touching the corners of parking lots, curling against the schools facing closure, the malls with empty space, the new university so peacock proud on its hill, teal feathers strutting. The scent of pulp: I remember my parents used to speak of Prince George, of people they once knew who lived in the city, of furniture infused with Prince George smell. Wherever they moved after Prince George, the city would follow them, follow them forever and beyond.

Three years after we arrived we have left again, and we miss it, awkwardly turning our faces to the sky with an expectation of pulp on the wind, missing the impossibly long winters and cold that freezes our lungs. We talk about it, describing the details of our meanderings, our snowshoeing across frozen lakes our giant northern dog swimming beside the canoe our friends happy to talk at length about gators and rain pants and the lack of jobs our trying to find books our frustration about the environment our understanding about the need to log and mine and drill for gas. You send us a letter and a card that reaches us in our new home. In the card you write about hearing, for the first time, the heartbeat of your baby. Do you remember you said you thought it was impossible for another life to be growing in the watery confines of your uterus? I think of calling you, trying to explain that I can almost hear the heartbeat too; that nothing is impossible because you live in a town carved haphazardly from the wilderness, a town with lungs filled with pulp air, veins pumping with rivers and glacier runoff, limbs held strong with the iron and steel of trucks and trains. I want to tell you no place could have been better for you to hear, for the first time, that heartbeat. I want to tell you that the heartbeat makes a town become a *there*, not an *away*, not an always searching for somewhere else; heartbeats allow us to see from the ground up rather than always looking down from above.

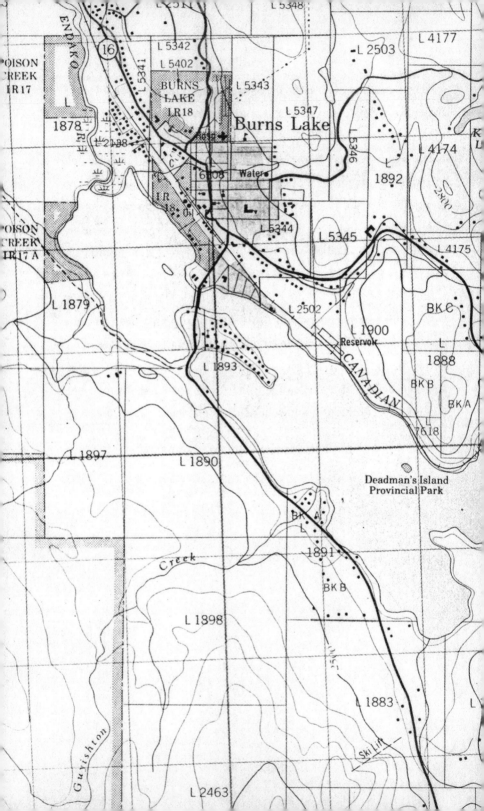

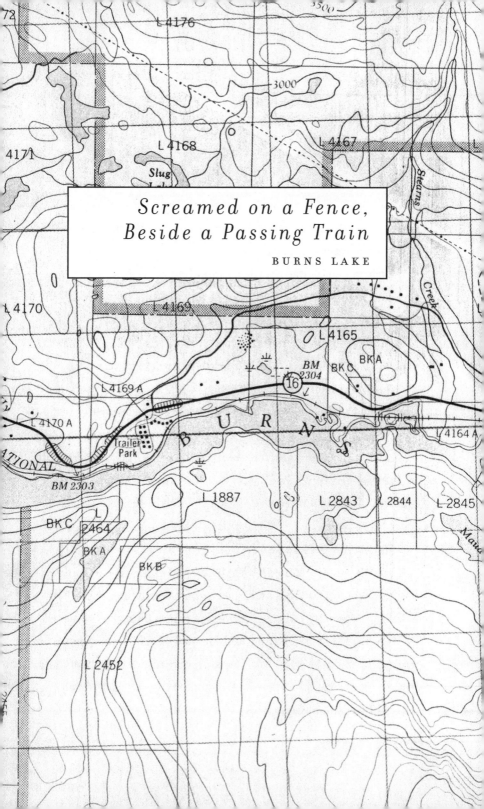

Screamed on a Fence, Beside a Passing Train

BURNS LAKE

IT HAS BEGUN TO RAIN. THE TRAIN WHISTLE BLOW-
ing, the conductor inside this CN passenger car selling a small wood
train whistle, and for a quick moment the two are in harmony, the
whistle outside, the wooden whistle inside, all around the sound of
train, we are encased in train.

Early this morning: a train station filled with seniors. Late winter and travels through the Rocky Mountains, passing through the
spines of mountains rippling under the weight of never-ending
snow and then into the foothills, waiting at a train station. This trip
is beginning, the sky still black though morning has arrived.

And now, just now: the clickidy-clack of a train crossing a
bridge, black bridge beam, landscape and river, black bridge beam,
landscape and river, black bridge beam . . . and we are over the
river, a frozen river with yellowed snow and ice, fat-like, layer of
insulation, protection resting on top. Red-osier dogwood bent into
water. Now the fields again, sloping into just the hint of mountains,
green everywhere once, but not now—only a desperate whisper of
what is waiting. Still grey and ochre.

I think we are somewhere outside Burns Lake—certainly the
landscape is one of lakes and rushes and cat tails, the bark of cottonwood trees so black, mountain ranges unto themselves, there is
the implication of fire, something burnt and left for spring. As if
winter burns, as if this landscape of fire scar has not yet fully
healed; Burns Lake, lake on fire, lake burning, the last remaining
tinder of tired flames.

The rain has stopped. The fractures of unfrozen space on the surfaces of lakes and ponds are no longer disrupted by millions of raindrops. They are smooth to face the winter sky.

We have passed several collections of wasted car bodies, shot at and spray-painted. I am envisioning a truck load of locals, Friday night and perhaps angry at parents, cases of beer, bottles of vodka, and the thin beauty of a shotgun, unlocked from someone's basement, almost forgotten, not viewed as anything beyond something to use on the odd weekend for target practice. Any other use of that gun has been disregarded.

Overhead there are now great washes of clear blue sky. Across an expanse of rolling hills a section of land is illuminated in isolation, a thick bar of brightness at odds with everything around it. We are passing sawmills, one outside my window now—West Fraser Forest Products, a collection of trailers, steam pouring out from great kiln dryers—smoke and sawdust making sure people are at work, able to make a living, bring home survival to their families, their families waiting at home, waiting for fathers smelling like steamed wood, like a forest on fire.

And the towns outside the train, small and grey-rusted metal and broken—balanced in such a huge landscape, desperately, impossibly, yet with such absolute conviction, and our train is moving past, moving into Burns Lake. To one side of the platform a wood sign, carved and painted with sure hands, well paid for, reading, "Welcome to Burns Lake, Gateway to Tweedsmuir Park." Across the platform another sign, neon surveying—tape letters knit into a chain-link fence, done in the careful, stitched hand of controlled fury, fury with nowhere else to go, ignited fire with nothing left to burn. Such an extensive fence, a fence long enough for everyone on the train to turn toward and read words screaming at a passing train, screaming at residents of Burns Lake and passers-by alike. INDIANS HAVE NO RIGHTS IN THIS TOWN—END APARTHEID NOW! YOU CAN CONTROL OUR WATER, BUT YOU CAN'T CONTROL OUR SOULS!

Turn your head. It makes no difference. Emblazoned bright even as you shut your eyes. The message cannot be ignored, and we are pulling away from the platform, passing a cemetery on the edge of town, this too encircled in a chain-link fence, old stone crosses and paint-peeling wind-polished grey wooden crosses facing a lake, just a stone's throw from the fence screaming. I am imagining souls, souls no one can capture, souls fighting for the rights they have had stolen, and we are pulling out of Burns Lake and the train is running fast on well-worn tracks. It does not have the time to stop for souls, for the land outside the windows, agricultural land and round corrals filled with mud caked horses. It could not stop each time the sandy land slopes down and touches the lake in exquisite quiet beauty, each time another grove of straight silver aspen grows up outside the window, or each time a bird with bright orange feet flashes into the tea coloured water open between ice flows.

Now outside the windows are flat grasslands with pine trees. Now another lumberyard, hydro and telephone poles, everything, each piece of wood stained green with a curing agent, forced uniformity. And the high, high piles of sawdust and woodchips, broken trees sprayed on snow. Perfect then, that the stop this train did make was met with such memorable brilliance, with bright words, a flash point burned on memory in Burns Lake, separating the homes of those whose water has been turned off by the municipality and the homes of those who turned it off.

For a moment, on this train, I was balanced between the two.

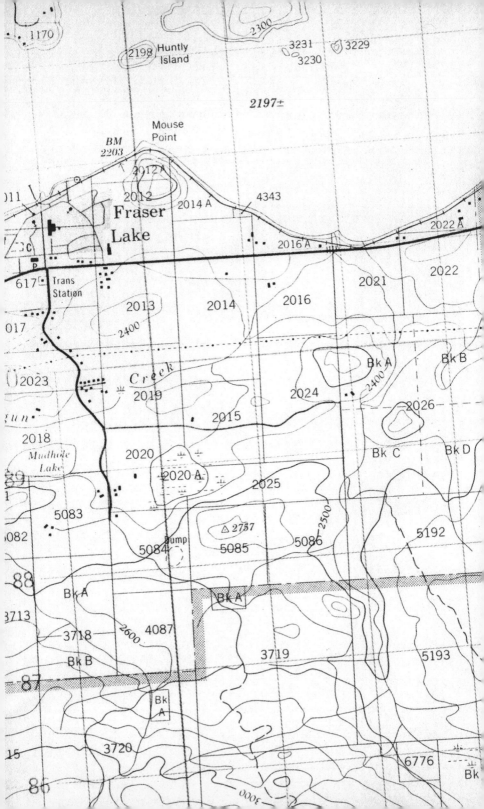

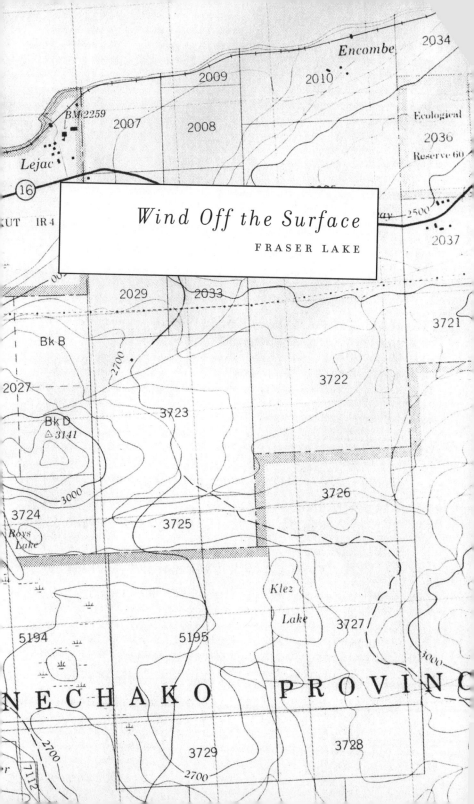

Wind Off the Surface

FRASER LAKE

THIS IS THE SITE OF YOUR SECOND HEARTBREAK.

It is not as clean as the first break, not as instantaneous or as sure. This does not mitigate the pain or the confusion, but it means the events unfold on a bedraggled organ—less a lightening strike and more a solid, unending rain, soaking and saturating every pore of the earth. Your heart is already a battleground. It mirrors the landscapes you have moved across back and forth, back and forth. As before, you did not foresee this break, and you could not anticipate its ripple effects throughout your life.

It began, in your childhood memory, on the day your father packed you, your brother, and your sister into the car, driving back roads outside of Kitwanga and having trouble getting to any point. He stops, pulls over, gets out to rummage in the trunk of the car, and reappears with arms laden down with fishing rods, tackle, and other gifts for your sister that you do not remember anymore. He explains about your mother's absence, about the decision for her to move so far away, back to the wheat fields, flatness and red earth of her native Oklahoma, back to near where you where born in New Mexico though you no longer remember that, now that rivers and mountains and the landscapes of northern British Columbia have firmly imprinted your being.

You know something is being hidden, but you are not sure what.

That will come. It will come in time, over time, against time, when you are older, and when you are not older but are wandering the streets of Fraser Lake on a Saturday afternoon, brother and sister in tow, your father and new stepmother locked away in a bedroom having told you all to entertain yourselves, to go on your merry way.

You are too preoccupied with the fishing rods to think of even next week, and you know nothing yet of Fraser Lake. But soon, even before you have the chance to slick the new rod's fishing line in a stream or lake, you will get to know the town of Fraser Lake; it will become a map you carry around on your heart forever. You might have left the region, the province, or the country for months, but even at the age of thirty you would have been able to find anything in Fraser Lake with your eyes shut. Some things stay with a twelve year old.

Leaving every Friday afternoon after school. Driving four and a half hours along Highway 16, your exhausted body in the backseat, your father's music filling the air, keeping time to the twists and curves in the road, you eating gas station dinners, the neon lights of highway convenience stores blinding in the early dark of late winter days, your stomach filled to the rocking motion caused by semis and rigs passing your car, the woof of shuddering air, and the fast, faster, fastest speed your father's windshield wipers as they work to remove rain and mud thrown from the massive tires of the passing transport truck.

Endako. You pass this nothing of a town on the way to Fraser Lake. Endako is where your new grandparents live, your new grandfather a miner from the open pit molybdenum mine, a crater more expansive than your entire life; it makes your stomach lurch, your throat constrict, and your cells hum when you stand on the lip of that mine, staring down, refusing to hold anyone's hand. They are your new family and you have no desire to connect with them. You once had the terrible thought of jumping, then thought better of it, thinking instead of pushing people. You do not think of death, only of the wonderful weightless feeling of being held by nothing but air, arms spread wide and full of horizon, the word your tongue trips over, molybdenum, suddenly a song called easily and without hesitation. You are dreaming nothing stands in your way, you are dreaming that the world, and every word that stitches it together, is yours. You can wrap your arms around it, pronounce it perfectly.

Of course it was impossible, but nonetheless you carried this vision with you in your roamings of Fraser Lake. During each of those countless and endless weekends when you walked the perimeter of the baseball diamond, every small northwestern town has a pitted and muddy diamond with sagging mesh behind the catcher's mound, during those long hours when you walked up and down the highway, parallel to the barbwire fencing that separated you from the sparse agricultural fields on the edge of Fraser Lake, throughout the Saturdays and Sundays that passed with you leaning into the wind off the lake, the sound of Canada geese at first faint and then splittingly loud, the only company you remember for such long stretches of time.

Fraser Lake is loneliness to you. An ache in your gut, a wrenching in your heart, sporadically interrupted with pinball games and foosball, handfuls of sweat-soaked candy bought with the small number of coins handed to you as you were ushered out each morning without ceremony. Without an understanding of the tiny cracks opening up around you as you walked the limited number of streets, across the railway tracks, beside the sphere-shaped and animal-like petroleum containers behind the two gas stations, alongside the dumpsters behind the hotel and the blue cinder block Chinese restaurant. Smells of pork and rice and vegetables your twelve-year-old mouth could not pronounce. But then, when would you need to? You did not go out for a late Saturday night dinner, not even once, not even as the surprise you fell asleep dreaming about, the streets of Fraser Lake quite outside your strange and intermittent bedroom, and the soles of your feet aching only slightly less than the back of your throat, your heart, your missing of family, of what you had before, and of what is epitomized in the silence of this small town, the wind strong off Fraser Lake and onto Fraser Lake the town.

Twice without your consent. A heart broken twice, scarred and unhealed in the steets of Fraser Lake.

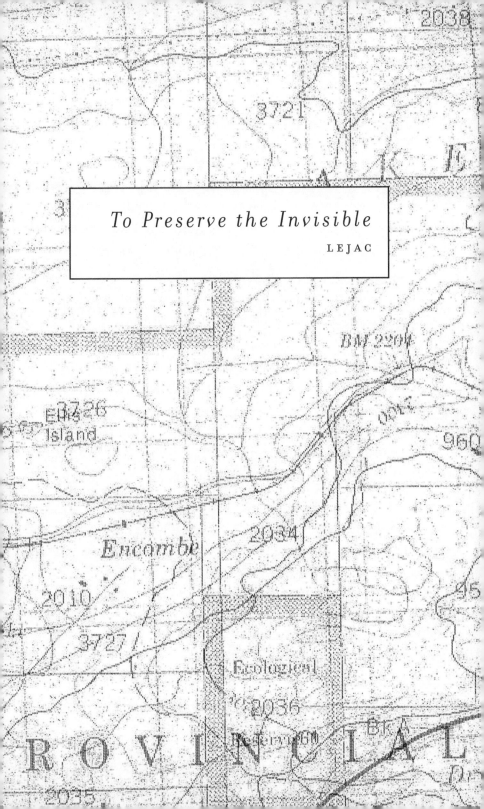

To Preserve the Invisible

LEJAC

ONLY HERE, IN THE EMPTINESS OF NOTHING BUT highway and lake, in the cruel vacuum of buildings destroyed and stories erased, in the inhaled scent of frost-covered grass. Only here, snow and ice and mud at the end of April, thin hawks striking at empty fields, stories of bears waking from hibernation and standing immobile, emaciated and waiting to die of starvation, their skin and fur baggy over bones, a winter so long that nothing has grown, nothing has breathed nor moved from this frozen state.

We are here because of your story, a story so fantastic and impossible I think for a moment you have made it up, invented spring for the sake of levity, imagined the absurd for the sake of my momentary awe. Last night you suggested we travel to your cabin on Francois Lake, and we drive through Vanderhoof, through Fort Fraser, along the lake and through Fraser Lake, through Endaco and past the pub, the railway houses, the gutted remains of mining equipment laced with frozen, exploded and spent cat-tail rushes, brittle and easy to break in any strong wind. I am driving your pickup truck, heater on, your laughter in the warmth winding with stories of people in a world of their own.

There, behind that driveway entrance, the one with moose antlers nailed high on burl-engulfed posts, that was the home of a man shot dead by his neighbour. It made the news, all over the province, this remote location the site of unspeakable anger, domestic abuse and incest, hunting and horses, men on the range fighting for women and honour and money and land. The story goes that his body lay frozen all

102

winter, was discovered by his horse and another rider during spring thaw, still cold but sunshine breaking through at last.

And that house, that house over there, it's owned by a Swiss family who faces deportation. They brought their daughter over to marry a local, wanting to get all their riches into Canada without paying taxes, needing a loophole and thinking marriage to a local would provide it. But there was confusion; money stolen, money unreported, and investigations were begun, families feuding on the shores of Francois Lake, famous for its Lake Char, famous for its great inland orientation of east to west thwarting the direction of other lakes. Cabins known for their owners, drunks who stumble home late, carpenters with an angel's touch for woodwork, families who have been on the lake since the dawn of time, microcosm of politics and perspectives intersecting with herds of deer, slips of agricultural land bending into the shores of the lake.

The night you tell me of Lejac, of possible sainthood bracketed by sawmills, reserves, and small town truck stops, you also tell me how to monitor your woodstove. How to keep track of the needle moving towards the red, of the valves that need to be opened carefully and with a sure stroke, of how to press log on log on log, filling up the space to ensure an even burn, heat throughout the night and into the cold of the following morning.

I do not tell you that I already know.

I like your story of sainthood interspersed with woodstove instructions; telling you that I am fluent in the monitoring of woodstoves, that I grew up beside great wood furnaces welded together from the fuel tanks of tugboats, telling you this would only interrupt the narrative, break the rhythmic waves of your meanderings through history and research and work to the tales of Lejac.

The next morning, a late April morning that has brought almost a foot of snow, the lake is white with snow refusing to melt, and the trees are quiet. A window has been broken in the shop behind your lakeside house, a circular break leaving two cruel shards of glass glinting in the snow, and we are concerned about coyotes cutting their tender, wild feet on glass, concerned about bats flying inside, unable to leave once their day of leather-winged sleep is finished. Together we clean up the glass, search the snow, even below the snow and into frozen soil thick with Hemlock needles. Without gloves my hands are red swollen cold, clumsy as I hammer plastic over the break, noticing for the first time two thin feathers caught on a shard still in place in the window frame.

There is no sense to timing, and as I remove those two delicate feathers from sharp and deadly glass, you suggest that on our return home we drive into Lejac, the site of Lejac Indian Residential School, now a site of pilgrimage, a site of documented miracle.

From the highway it is invisible. Not long ago, the structures still stood; the brick school house, the outbuildings, the barns and sheds and the separate homes for priests and teachers. Now, nothing but a water silo is visible from the highway, a marred egg-shape held in place by decaying iron. On old maps you see the buildings, the site depicted as populated, mute with regard to the pain of the residing population.

A thin but militaristically straight road intersects Highway 16; driving east you turn left off the highway, right where the road ends, and before you, opened up and stretched taut, a field encircled by twelve tall crosses. And on this evening the wind is cruel and loud, crying against the lakeshore, beating at the edges of a cemetery contained by a white picket fence, contained in the great open field, picturesque and neighbourly. Do you know, I am asked, how they made this field? and I answer, no, how is a field made? By chaining together young Native men, boys, children, chaining them together and hitching ploughs to them, leather straps not for a moment slack; they would work like mules, clearing the stumps and complex root systems of trees, breaking the soil and making it arable, levelling the ground, opening their bodies, sowing the wheat. On this frozen day the grass is golden, moving in the wind it sounds like glass shattering far away, smooth, the field is smooth. Something one might take pride in, wilderness conquered. And there, you tell me, over there, as you open the gate leading me inside the cemetery, facing me, a crucifix against the sky, framed by field, there, to the left, those small wooden crosses are the only marked graves of children and babies who died in the Lejac Indian Residential School.

Landscape transformed, marked.

My feet ache with the touch of a field whispering around me, sighing out the possibilities of bones never discovered, pain and grass, grass and pain. What might remain unmarked.

We turn, facing towards the south end of this cemetery, and you show me the reason we have come, the reason I come to learn that thousands of people converge on this site every year, people from around the world, strangers in a strange field. Only here, the hedge touching field touching fence touching highway leading east to a sawmill. Saint against sawmill, marked along Highway 16 and easy to pass.

Her grave is ornamented. A carved headstone, the faces of

porcelain angels muddy and only barely keeping afloat on top of snow drifts, the silk petals of artificial roses and irises garish in this stark and cruel landscape. Prayer beads, artificial pearls, shellac now peeling, are wrapped around her headstone.

The headstone of Rose Prince of the Carrier Nation, possible saint.

The decision is still out. Two documented miracles attributed to this First Nations woman, magnet of the Catholic world, symbol of possible healing, fractures mending, fissures closing. It was three years after she died that her casket had to be moved. In the fifties, people elsewhere were discovering dishwashers and fuel injection. Here, against a horizon dominated by the brick of an active residential school, the body of Rose Prince is being moved. Her casket was lifted and exposed once again to sky and wind and the sound of movements in trees. In the process of moving the casket, it broke open, and Rose the Carrier tumbled out, perhaps her palms towards this field, this field created on the backs and blood of boys.

A miracle, a true miracle, for the body of Rose Prince was perfectly preserved, a halo of sweet scent permeating the air, and it is after this first miracle that a second occurred, a man whose back has been permanently disfigured and caused him never-ending pain, this man was touched with soil from the grave of Rose Prince, and he is healed. During the more than fifty years since her death, the hush of Rose Prince, possible saint, has erupted into a near roar, the roar of motor homes thundering on pilgrimages along Highway 16, the high whine volume of sound-system feedback distortion as crowds gather each summer, announcements made. All signs of Lejac Indian Residential School have been removed; not a single brick remains to

be found in the tall grasses surrounding the cemetery containing
Rose Prince. A swing set remains, abandoned, the soft hues of pink,
purple, yellow, and green in contrast to boys harnessed like mules.

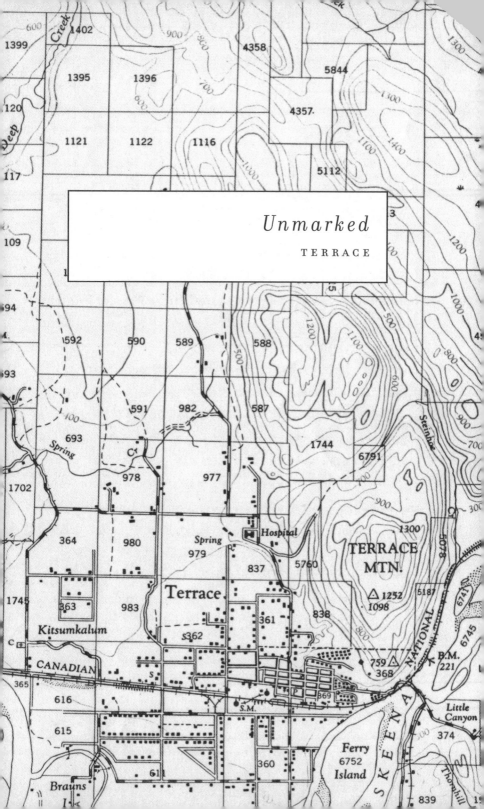

Unmarked

TERRACE

PRACTICE. IN THE BEGINNING, IN THAT FIRST YEAR, it was practice. It set the stage for years of moving to, from, and through logging towns, towns forever balanced on the edge of wilderness, on the edge of their very reason for existence. It was preparation, preparation for how to dream of escape, dream of everywhere but here, dream of endless motion when you are anchored in absolute immobility. A year-long dress rehearsal for adolescence in a town with the dubious honour of having the highest teen pregnancy rate in the province, an adolescence of watching bar fights and getting drunk on the edge of clear-cuts, in gravel pits, behind truck stops.

Anywhere but here.

Did it make me any more resilient, any stronger? Did it prime my pallet for a fluency in the languages of rural communities?

I really cannot say.

Images of northern resource communities have resided within me from a time prior to memory. Never have long winters stretching between September and May not been known. Never has daylight beginning at 8:30 in the morning and vanishing by 3:30 in the afternoon not been a part of how I understand the day and night. This is not to suggest such a time did not exist. Indeed it did, only it was a time before I was one year old, and thus a time I have no memory of. In 1974, just days before my first birthday, my parents moved north for the first time.

I do not remember, but my parents tell me I discovered the moon just past Meziaden Junction near the boarder with Alaska, six hours north of Terrace by gutted logging road, and two and half hours southeast of Stewart. At that time, Stewart was a booming mining town, houses being built just as fast as miners and their families moved in. Apartment blocks sprang up within metres of terminal glaciers. A community civic centre, complete with a swimming pool, took its place beside gold rush hotels. I discovered the moon from the back seat of a car driving logging roads to a mining town, my father hired on contract work to assess fish-bearing streams standing in the way of road construction plans. In the same way the moon cannot be attributed to a moment of discovery in my memory, the landscapes of northern British Columbia are not reducible to a particular point of discovery in my memory. Both the landscapes of northern British Columbia and the moon are intrinsic to me, as subconscious and necessary as breathing, as a heartbeat.

Between 1974 and 1975 we lived in the Cedars Motel. Two bedrooms, a kitchen, and a living room whose front window balanced on the shoulder of Highway 16, looking over into the mill yards—into lumber sorts and squares of muddy soil upon which newly milled two-by-fours rested before being loaded on trains headed for the coast. I teethed to the sounds of logging trucks and boxcars, toilet trained in a motel for men in from camp on their days off. As a baby, the sounds of a logging town coaxed and rocked me to sleep, the sounds of pickup trucks and loggers telling stories all filtered through thin motel walls.

Stories have become memories, truth and fiction inseparable. The stories told to me of our year in the Cedars Motel have implanted themselves so firmly in my sense of the world that it is as if they are my own, always my own, as if the details of stories are remembered details and not ones imagined. Brief flashes do exist of my own memories, memories not culled and assembled from people's stories, but my own memories are always braided securely with details known only from other people's stories. It is forever a question: Is this a memory or an image solidified from years of hearing a story?

The flash of recollection—acquiring a cat. My father away on a moose hunting trip and my mother and I alone in our motel home. Memory begins with the knock on the door and a small girl standing there from the Kitsumkalum reserve down the highway. In her arms she is holding a box of kittens. Her mother has told her that working-men in from camp like to bring things like kittens back to their families. Her mother has told her that these kittens will find good homes if the girl gives them away to men staying in motels. Ours is the first door she knocks on, and my father is not home, only my mother and me. My mother takes one nonetheless, naming it Moose with the hopes that my father will return quickly. When he phones, my mother tells him there is no need to shoot a moose, he can come home right away. We already have a moose, she says. I am playing with her right now, on the pale green carpet of our motel home living room carpet.

In 1974, my father has told me, moose meat was still a core component of diets in northern British Columbia. Moose meat and fish, jars of canned salmon or freezers of fish, augmented a diet of canned vegetables and potatoes. Bread was baked at home because Terrace did not yet have a bakery and store-bought bread was rare, often already mouldy when the truck came in. Fresh fruits and vegetables were almost non-existent, save for the high months of summer when they made splash appearances at the one grocery store or appeared at a local farmers's market.

A time existed when red peppers, avocadoes, or green leaf lettuce were as rare to Terrace residents as the eagles we regularly witnessed pulling steelhead from rivers were to our southern counterparts. Terrace practiced becoming a town, taking its first baby steps towards becoming a city.

Know, now, that in this story many years have passed.

We left Terrace long ago, but it drew my parents back, surrounded by mountains and river, salmon berry bushes rustling in wind, the fine tendrils of silver green lichen reaching from high red cedar boughs to the ground—always back to this northern ground. From the child I was in the Cedar's Motel, my limbs now ache with the effort of growing tall, adolescence bursting out of me, unknown to me, known to you who grows to know everything about me, who later knows me better than I know myself. In my mind we have walked every street here, explored the spaces of every lumberyard and railway station, snuck home on every trail and back alley. It is as if I learned Terrace from you. After all, we knew the northern lights from their appearance over your back yard.

My first Monday of school away from the Queen Charlotte Islands—it is as if my vision has become a wide-angle lens. Everything is large beyond the imagination. A high school with more than six rooms. Stoplights and pedestrian cross walks, things I had not known in over seven years. I have come from nothingness to this, am hesitant to cross a road, the traffic terrifying. This is huge and dangerous and impossible to navigate. Crossing the threshold to a homeroom at school is like being hit by a truck. By grade ten I had not yet attended a homeroom. What for? In Queen Charlotte City we all knew home. Everyone knew us, we were each accounted for and no need existed to check us in, to route us through homeroom

In the space of that newness of homeroom, the first question you asked me is, "where do you live?" Confusing, as I remained rooted in Queen Charlotte City, still balanced on the edge of the Pacific Ocean. Then, with quick remembrance, I re-locate myself, answering absurdly "here, I live here." It is your patience with my ineptness that bonds us, your rewording, asking me, "what street is your house on here in Terrace?" Allowing me to place myself in this new town, my new home.

We told ourselves, told each other, told stories to keep alive and to propel us forward day by day by day. We created our fictions to survive. We envisioned red lines charting our every movement. New travels were made permanent in our heads by envisioning an etching of red across a map of Terrace. The map was carefully folded inside our minds, a map of roads and hills and lengths of times to walk home; a map of under bridges and beside the lake hoping desperately not to get pregnant. A map of just how to navigate being an adolescent in a place like Terrace. A map of how to navigate it together.

Look here. Look closely. Where the industrial section webs out, where the highway crosses the railway tracks, where real estate prices divide one side of town from the other. Where they put the welfare offices, "just so people did not have so far to walk." So people in poverty would stay on their own side. The first time we crossed the tracks together it was just east of the downtown Skeena Cellulose mill. On any map other than the one we carried inside ourselves, inside our heads, the crossing is impossible to demarcate. In our mind maps, though, the site was perfectly clear.

We are weaving through the boxcars, hands greasy black from grasping jointed joining cables, something close to joy aching in our throats. We are, after all, thwarting death. Already, two train mechanics have been killed on these tracks, and the terribleness of disobeying orders is sweeter with the clutch of a truly awful image lodged clearly in our minds. Another night (this has by now become habit, all sound eclipsed while standing in the chasms between box cars, a wonderful thrill of entrapment as one line of cars lurches into motion, deafening) we climbed into the open car. Lay in great piles of wood chips headed west for Prince Rupert and then Japan. We charted an escape plan anchored in wood chip cars, across the Pacific Ocean, anything to leave this town, anything to flee.

Flee what? From what did we imagine ourselves running?

Oh, our lists were long and carefully organized. We aimed to escape every cinder block business, every lack that was nothing to do, no one to see. We had plans to escape every teenage death and every accident, every teenage pregnancy and every shut down, laid-off, out of work, depressed, and trapped resident who filtered in through the edges of our understandings about home. When plans to flee faltered, when we spent money from after school jobs on vodka rather than bus tickets and savings accounts, when we fell in love with the sons of mill workers and truck drivers, when we caught ourselves thinking about liking Terrace (buying a house, taking out a car loan—this was what the grade twelve graduates ahead of us were doing), when we caught ourselves (or caught each other) doing any of these things, we played the role of reminder.

We bore bad news to each other.

Consider the rafting accident with Sheri Davidson. Sixteen years old and partying with three guys in town just for the summer, work-ing on the highways, working construction and flagging, driving graders and shovelling tar. Three guys over thirty and out for a good time, happy to buy the beer, happy to drive down to the river, pump up the tubes on a hot Saturday afternoon. Tie the inner tubes together, float down the Kalum River, cooler of beer anchored in a net dragging deep below the water's surface.

Remind each other.

Of Sheri's cousin Daisy who watched Sheri being dragged under the logjam, Daisy who watched Sheri disappear, her body never to be found. Remind each other; remind each other of the rafting trips we'd been invited on, of the nights in trucks with drunken highway and construction workers.

Consider Crystal, same grade as me, killed when her boyfriend drove his Chevy truck into her, breaking her body against the wall of the Greyhound Bus Station. Remind each other of how one of the only two Chinese restaurants in town closed shortly thereafter, the connected restaurant's inside wall shared with the bus station.

Consider the two suicides, both hangings, both young First Nations men (why not be honest? In school everyone called them Indians, slurring the syllables, mocking the accent—this is what they were to everyone. Indians). They seemed ephemeral to us, as if they did not exist—fleetingly they were bussed in from out of town reserves, caught only on the edges of our vision, our bodies, because in schools clear divisions had been created, territories mapped out with the confines of halls and locker rows. Skid row, where the Indians hung out at break and lunch, reservation alley, where we caught ourselves not looking.

Consider the four girls in my grade ten year alone who left school, forbidden to attend because of "the condition of pregnancy." In a class of less than one hundred, their absences were considerable, the whispers of their lives deafening.

Consider waiting on Friday afternoon for a truck of friends driving to Terrace from Prince Rupert. Along the banks of the Skeena River, that narrow, twisting Highway 16 paralleled on one side by river, on the other by cliff and railway track. Waiting for hours, well past any explicable time delays, and then the call to a parent in Prince Rupert; confusion and a call to the RCMP.

Remind each other of the tiny slip of wheel, a misplaced stone, and the near death of two. Cherry, a face rebuilt with metal plating (medical miracle after the impact with the truck's stick shift), and Tom, the one travelling to see you, left with the endless searching for marks and bruises it seemed impossible to have not sustained.

Long after we have moved away from Terrace, we contemplate not having the scars and bruises inflicted upon others in our grades, in our town. As best friends, we searched each other, then painfully congratulated each other for escaping.

While there, we considered carefully—reminded each other in the back seats of cars racing down main street past the only two grocery stores, past the one men's clothing store, the one shoe store, the hotel. We reminded each other as we learned to drive winding logging gravel roads outside of town, as we downed bootlegged bottles of rye whiskey in empty fields, as we skipped school to cower in the corner booths of a steak house, drinking coffee and imagining ourselves older, beautifully citified.

Everything we dreamt was away. Everywhere we imagined ourselves was somewhere other than here.

Here was the movie theatre with gold shag carpet walls, with fea-ture presentations five months behind everywhere else. Here was a centre of town with beehive burners rather than skyscrapers, muse-ums, nightclubs, or the imagined endless options that existed in the city. Beehive burner, glowing hot orange pink, throwing flames like mountain ranges into the sky, illuminating nothing but log sorts and box cars. Here was the kind of place invisible on televisions, invisi-ble in school texts unless mentioned as "rural places where men worked hard and life was difficult." Oh how we ached to race toward *there*, the infinite *there* that was anywhere but the unmarked here.

ACKNOWLEDGEMENTS

This book started many years ago in an effort to articulate the landscapes of northwestern British Columbia, the landscapes I know as
home. Over those years I have had the very great pleasure of never
working entirely alone on the project. As a consequence, I owe my
deepest gratitude to many people who have offered me their guidance, their support, and their friendship.

I am grateful to my editor Taiaiake Alfred, who was both generous
in his guidance and motivating with his suggestions. Ruth Linka and
Rebecca Whitney of NeWest Press have been wonderful in their
thoughtfulness and attention to detail. A number of people have been
teachers and mentors to me during the writing of this book: I wish to
extend a heartfelt thank you to Julia Emberly, Gail Fondahl, Robert
Budde, Kevin Hutchins, Stephen Hume, and Lawrence McCann.

Family and friends are the foundations of any landscape, and I
owe a great debt to my partner, Luke Eades, to my parents, Mary
and Dionys de Leeuw, and to an inspirational group of people I am
privileged to know as friends, including Allison Sivak, Carmen
Ellison, Renee Prasad, Kevin Knox, Jodi West, Jess and John Dafoe,
Debbie Scarborough, Christiana Wiens, Melissa Munn, Deb Thien,
Mary MacDonald and Steve Lang, Jill Stockburger, and Margo
Greenwood. These people ensure that I fully appreciate the truth of
that omnipresent observation that a book is never, ever, an indi-
vidual project.

SARAH DE LEEUW grew up in Duncan, The Queen Charlotte Islands (Haida Gwaii), and Terrace, BC. After de Leeuw earned her BFA from the University of Victoria she spent time teaching English in South Korea. She has also worked as a tug boat driver, logging camp cook, a journalist and correspondent for *Connections Magazine*, CBC's *BC Almanac*, and, most recently, as the Research Coordinator for the University of Northern British Columbia's task force on the effects of substance abuse on children. De Leeuw earned her Masters degree from UNBC and is currently working on her PhD in Cultural Geography at Queen's University in Kingston, Ontario.